At last, after almost three decades of hearing Christian educators lamenting the absence of a solid, biblically faithful resource for teaching digital citizenship, Ben Boche and Jake Hollatz step up to the challenge and offer this precious gift to pastors, parents, and especially Christian educators around the world.

Dr. Bernard Bull, Vice Prov...
Innovation at Concordia U...
Digitized: Spiri... ... *Technology*

Faithfully Connected provides a road map to be safe, savvy, faith-filled digital citizens on the information highway. This resource incorporates God's Word, highlights articles of confession, and brings to focus the essential questions needed for faith development in the digital age. With clarity like a catechism and practical, user-friendly lesson plans, Jake Hollatz and Ben Boche have created a timely text to help leaders facilitate discussions and learners to fully contemplate their identity as digital citizens. This book will help everyone comprehend their roles more deeply as Christians who are called to be "in this world but not of this world."

James G. Rush II, English (EFL) Instructor,
Luther University—Yongin, South Korea

In *Faithfully Connected*, authors Jake and Ben methodically match biblical principles to today's key digital challenges for young people. They delve into what is so challenging about growing up digital and then show class room teachers, pastors, layleaders, and parents how to prepare children with the skills and traits of godly citizens for a future we can't predict. Both in their presentation of the challenges and in their preparation of classroom and catechism lessons, Jake and Ben demonstrate how connected they are to today's Lutheran classrooms, their students, their communities, and the state of our digitally absorbed world.

Tim Schumacher, Assistant Professor of Educational
Technology, Concordia University Irvine

A must-read for Lutheran educators as we embrace digital technology with Christian character and integrity! With media and digital technology ever present in our lives, *Faithfully Connected* provides the resources to teach and model digital citizenship with Christian character. The nine common traits presented serve as a useful and powerful guide to teach children and young adults how to be immersed as digital citizens in a meaningful, purposeful, and responsible manner. Great resource with invaluable essential questions, teaching tips, and lesson plans!

Sharon Frydendall, Middle School Teacher,
St. John's Lutheran School
Orange, CA

Teaching our students digital citizenship in our schools and parishes is an essential responsibility that we have as Christian educators. *Faithfully Connected* is an excellent resource for any teacher or pastor who wants to empower their students to be faithful ambassadors of Christ in their increasingly digital world. The authors' faithful connection to Christian school curriculum and the catechism are an essential component as we equip the next generation of believers.

Jonathan P. Orr, LAT, ATC, MEd, Director of Innovation
and Continuous Improvement, Faith Lutheran Middle School
& High School

Something that many Lutheran and Christian educators have been asking about for years is a manageable and up-to-date way to effectively teach digital citizenship in their classrooms. *Faithfully Connected* fills that need in a very timely and relevant manner by connecting the very students being taught with the lessons and methodology of what it means to be a Christian living in today's digital world. The inclusion of well-explained and easy-to-use lesson plans gives educators the tools they need to teach such an important topic, regardless of their "digital" comfort level. *Faithfully Connected* will fill a need both now and in the years to come!

Matthew Bergholt, LCMS School Ministry

Drawing from research, personal experience, and the voices of students, Boche and Hollatz have created a resource that will add value to a variety of audiences. Exploring topics ranging from digital access to rights and responsibilities, this book will challenge your assumptions about living in a digital age while uncovering what it means to be a faith-filled digital citizen. Parents, pastors, and educators alike will benefit from this text—which, in turn, will bless the students they serve.

Heath Lewis, MA, DCE, Instructor in Christian Education,
DCE Program Director, Department
of Theology and Ministry
Concordia University St. Paul

FAiThfully
CONNECTEd

INTEGRATING BIBLICAL PRINCIPLES IN A DIGITAL WORLD

BEN BOCHE AND JAKE HOLLATZ

CONCORDIA PUBLISHING HOUSE · SAINT LOUIS

Published by Concordia Publishing House
3558 S. Jefferson Avenue, St. Louis, MO 63118-3968
1-800-325-3040 · cph.org

Manufactured in the United States of America

Library of Congress Cataloging-in-Publication Data

Names: Boche, Ben, author, Hollatz, Jake, author.

Title: Faithfully connected : integrating biblical principles in a digital
    world / by Ben Boche and Jake Hollatz.

Description: St. Louis : Concordia Publishing House, 2018.

Identifiers: LCCN 2017048963 (print) | LCCN 2017059707 (ebook) | ISBN
    9780758659552 | ISBN 9780758659545

Subjects: LCSH: Technology--Religious aspects--Christianity--Study and
    teaching. | Christianity and culture--Study and teaching. | Digital
    communications--Study and teaching. | Digital media--Religious
    aspects--Christianity--Study and teaching.

Classification: LCC BR115.T42 (ebook) | LCC BR115.T42 B63 2018 (print) | DDC
    261.5/2--dc23

LC record available at https://lccn.loc.gov/2017048963

---

1 2 3 4 5 6 7 8 9 10   27 26 25 24 23 22 21 20 19 18

Table of Contents

"How we get along in our digital community"

DIGITAL CITIZENSHIP

"I think citizenship is being good to people who live all around you in your community and nice to people around you, like your neighbor. Digital citizenship, then, is being nice to people and thinking about how we get along in our digital community. For example, there is a community in the online gaming world and on social media. You should also be respectful and smart online and have a general self-awareness when you are online. This means recognizing the right and wrong way to behave online. Faith Digital Citizenship means being a good representative of Jesus. As a Christian, when we are online, we should treat others with respect and not say bad words. We should also show God's mercy and grace to others. The bottom line is that we should use digital and online technology to grow in our faith and not destroy it."

LIFE IN THE twenty-first century has become integrated in fundamental ways. Home heating and air conditioning can be controlled remotely. Our vehicles can be started via a key fob for early heating or cooling. We can speak with our friends and family over the phone, with text messages, and with video chats. Questions can be answered by Google, Siri, Alexa, or Cortana. The primary strand that integrates all of these everyday conveniences is technology. Advances in technology have enabled our lives to be integrated or connected with others around us, from shopping experiences to learning.

It is a rare experience to walk into a school classroom in any type of community and not find technology that enables learning to reach out further than it ever has. Gone are the days of the *Encyclopedia Britannica* volumes sitting on a classroom or library shelf. They have been replaced by the current realities of Discovery Education streaming, Wikipedia, and About.com integrated into common Internet searches. To make information searching even easier, students are using smartphones and other mobile technology to integrate instant information gathering into everyday learning experiences.[1]

Even though our lives have been completely permeated by technology, the vast majority of the population interacting with the new technological realities are still digital immigrants.[2] As we grapple with moving from traditional twentieth-century roles for learning, communicating, and shopping (to name but a few of a growing list), we simultaneously are embracing the conveniences of twenty-first-century technology. Smartphones with a multitude of apps seem to be replacing common tasks like shopping, navigation, and talking to our neighbors or friends. The complete impact of a world with technology that integrates into our everyday

---

1 See Maguth, "Educative Potential of Cell Phones."
2 See Prensky, "Digital Natives, Digital Immigrants: Part 1."

experience is somewhat unclear. However, we must recognize that it is changing the way we think, act, learn, and believe.

Rather than simply letting technology change and sometimes control the way we think, act, learn, and believe, we must be proactive not only in how we use technology, but also in how we view its role in our lives. What kind of environment—both offline and online—do we want to be a part of and even create? Where do our Christian beliefs and practices fit in and affect what we do with technology? Citizenship can define our identity—whether it's national, digital, or faith-related. For us as Christians, our identity and most important citizenship is in Christ.

At the core of a Christian's life is the belief in Jesus Christ as the Son of God and Savior of the world. While some may not immediately agree that technology has changed this core belief, technology has certainly provided a platform to ask more questions and challenge more common assumptions than has been done in the past. Technology often claims to be a panacea for problems rather than a partner in finding solutions. Our hope is that, through a careful and critical integration of faith and technology, we can be confident that technology becomes a help rather than a hindrance for Christians in all aspects of life, but especially in learning environments both formal and informal.

What does it mean to be a digital citizen?

Author, speaker, and educator Mike Ribble describes digital citizenship as "the norms of appropriate, responsible technology use."[3] While this simple definition is easy to remember, it does not bind together the realities of technology use in today's world. When we consider how integrated technology is in all aspects of modern life, knowing how to use technology appropriately is far more complicated. As a citizen of a particular city, state, or country, we have certain responsibilities. Following the laws and obeying local regulations is certainly a part of citizenship; however, following commonly accepted social norms and appropriate behavior toward fellow citizens is also essential to a citizenry that can live in

---

3 "Home Page," Digital Citizenship (website).

peace together. The same holds true for technology use. How we behave as citizens in the digital realm directly affects the peace of the digital society. The difficulty is that citizenship in today's postmodern or post-Christian society often puts the focus on ourselves, our relationships, and our "stuff" rather than on our Creator. True peace, therefore, is found only in salvation that comes from Jesus Christ. Our citizenship is built around our identity, and it is essential that we root our identity in Christ rather than in other aspects of culture and society.

KEY FEATURES

A critical piece to a responsible and peaceful citizenry is a common set of accepted rules or norms that everyone can agree on. Mike Ribble identified nine common traits for a healthy and successful digital citizenship:[4]

1. Digital access
2. Digital commerce
3. Digital communication
4. Digital literacy
5. Digital etiquette
6. Digital law
7. Digital rights and responsibilities
8. Digital health and wellness
9. Digital security

While these nine traits are not comprehensive to every digital situation, they cover the major areas of digital use. This approach allows us to develop a common goal. The common goal of citizens of the United States could be summed up by the concluding words of the Pledge of Allegiance: "Liberty and justice for all." Many Christian churches have common creeds that help form critical tenets of the faith. The common goal for Christians in digital citizenship is to use the technology God gave us in the most God-pleasing way possible, while rooting our identity in Him.

---

4 "Home Page," Digital Citizenship (website).

KNOWLEDGE BUILDING

Since creation, God has set humankind as the stewards of His creation. Technology is also a part of creation, and we are charged with using it wisely. When technology began downsizing and the personal computer emerged for everyday use, our society began transitioning to the digital realm. We had our first taste of integrated technology usage. As we have experienced, that usage has grown exponentially over the last thirty years. The need to use digital technology appropriately has also grown. It is estimated that 30 percent of the Internet is used solely for pornography.[5] That staggering amount is realization enough that we must be constantly aware of the digital environment around us and how it is used.

According to some sources, the amount of information available on the Internet doubles every twelve months, and some estimate that it will soon double every twelve hours.[6] This massive amount of information is hard to understand, yet we must attempt to manage it wisely. Schools and teachers are charged with building knowledge and encouraging the love of learning in school. Schools and teachers also have the complicated task of deciding the base of knowledge that students should know by heart and when it is more appropriate to know simply how to access information as needed. Consider the examples of previous technology compared with today's version:

- Road map ⟶ dashboard-mounted GPS ⟶ mobile phone
- Paper and pencil ⟶ typewriter ⟶ computer ⟶ Google Docs
- Telegraph ⟶ telephone ⟶ texting ⟶ video calling
- Chalkboard ⟶ whiteboard ⟶ Smartboard ⟶ interactive displays
- Abacus ⟶ slide rules ⟶ calculators

While the modes of learning technology have changed greatly, the final product has not changed. Learners in this age must continue to create and contribute knowledge rather than just consume information.

---

5 Enough Is Enough, "Pornography."
6 Schilling, "Knowledge Doubling."

AWARENESS

Creating knowledge and avoiding rampant consumerism in today's technology-driven world requires keen awareness of the digital environment. Educators must first be aware that all of the students they teach are technology natives and have grown up surrounded by smart technology, i-everything, and instant search results. While those advancements are well-intentioned, they have created some learners who expect all results to be lightning fast and gratifying. The other difficulty is that while students may know how to use digital technology proficiently for tasks like socializing with others, researching places to eat, and shopping, they do not always know how to use technology for academic purposes. Helping students recognize this awareness can change the learning environment. For example, students must be aware that not all quick answers are reliable, true, or God-pleasing.

Developing this keen awareness for technology does not happen automatically in life, nor is there a set curriculum for teaching it. Digital citizenship seeks to provide common language and interaction in digital environments so that all users can have an experience that is enlightening and productive. This awareness can also help give specific language to the images and actions that are appropriate and inappropriate in the online environment. When users have the ability to identify and call out content that is not appropriate, know what kinds of skills are needed to create websites, or recognize when it is time to get off of technology, we begin building that common understanding necessary for productive citizenship.

What does it mean to be a faith citizen?

The digital environment is easy to see all around us each day, but we must not forget that we are living in God's creation, we are under His care, and we have been created for His purposes. There is a common phrase among some Christians: We are in this world, but not of this world. This simple phrase alludes to an understanding that as believers in the risen Christ, we have residency in this world, yet have citizenship in a far better place with Christ.

Throughout the Bible, God's desire has been for us to identify with His authority rather than with the authorities or nations of this world. God's promises to Noah, Abraham, and Isaac were to build a great nation through them and their descendants (Genesis 17). This great nation became Israel. Being a citizen of the nation of Israel also meant being part of God's covenant people. Later on, in God's plan, He sent His Son, Jesus, to extend citizenship in that covenant community to the Gentiles. Because of Jesus' life, death, and resurrection, all people of the world have access to citizenship in the Father's kingdom. Belonging to God through the water and Word is part and parcel of being a faith citizen in the eternal realms of the triune God.

However, being a citizen of God's kingdom does not remove our residency in the current world. Those who are believers in Christ have a unique view of the world that God has given us. We are bound to Christ through our faith. That common faith is bound and formed in a variety of ways. The Lutheran view of our common faith is often summarized in the tenets of faith alone, grace alone, and Scripture alone. This faith view affirms the Christian belief and Lutheran doctrine that we are saved by faith alone, because of God's grace through faith in the inerrant Word of God. This common declaration of faith binds together those who believe. For centuries, those who believe in common elements of faith have grown together in their faith and work to make the best of the world around them.

We have both a vertical and a horizontal relationship with God. Our horizontal relationship with God consists of all that He has given us here on earth. This includes the technology that has become so important to most people today. The vertical relationship with God is our personal relationship with Him that we have received through our Baptism. Both of these aspects tie Lutheran Christians together in a common citizenship with God the Father. When we learn and grow together in a faith community, we are faith citizens. We are drawn together in shared experiences for the purpose of learning and growing together and being drawn closer to the triune God. Moreover, when the Holy Spirit draws us closer to Jesus through the work of Holy Baptism and the Lord's Supper, our purpose and citizenship are found in being children of God and thus striving to abide by God's will.

What does it mean to be a faith-filled digital citizen?

Citizenship is typically something that is a source of pride within a community. Communities that share in common beliefs and practices rally around one another for support and encouragement. In natural disasters, communities come together to help one another and recover. In times of celebration, people come together to cheer on their favorite sports team or congratulate a victory. A citizenship built around common beliefs and practices can accomplish far more than disparate individuals.

Spreading the Gospel of Jesus Christ is but one accomplishment that could not be done without a community of believers. The Early Christian Church knew that spreading the Good News could best be accomplished through a community with shared beliefs and common experiences. The same is true today in our digital society. The Gospel can be spread over technology, translated by technology, and stored in technology, but that can only happen when people come together in community. Part of our calling as Christians is to tell others about Jesus, and we do that as faith-filled citizens of God's kingdom.

As followers of Jesus, faith-filled digital citizens have a calling or vocation to abide by the common practices of our faith. Our vocation as Christians does not end at the conclusion of a church service; rather, we take our faith into the world for all to see. In the digital environment, our faith can take multiple forms and should be seen through our interactions online. The familiar song "They Will Know We Are Christians by Our Love" makes a point to mention that we affect others with our actions. Our digital interactions should be no different.

As a community of educators, parents, and teachers come together to help students grow in a variety of ways, this partnership is another area of citizenship or community that is affected by technology. The immense amount of information available to any individual can make it seem like teachers of all kinds are not necessary. However, as parents and teachers know, having information and using information are two separate things. Children and adults living in today's digital environment need input from fellow learners to help them grow in faith and knowledge. The digital environment is massive and can be treacherous, but when a community comes together in common faith and purpose, that environment does not have to be so overwhelming.

Because of the enormity and ambiguity of the digital realm, glorifying God through it is not an easy task. But that should not stop educators in their quest to display Christian faith in all environments of life. Whether it is the golden rule or "Love your neighbor as yourself," citizens of faith and citizens of the digital world must seek to do good in all circumstances, digital and physical.

Why should educators care about digital literacy and faith integration?

While doing good in all areas of life is noble, we know that we will fail. That is when we rely on Christ's forgiveness and power. In the professional sense, teachers are educators, but for our purposes, parents are also educators, and both teachers and parents must be ready to help our students and children through the trials and difficulties of living in a digital environment. Throughout the following chapters, we will outline the nine digital citizenship traits and how we can successfully integrate biblical principles and faith elements with each trait. It is important to notice that we do not separate our faith lives from our digital lives. The early Christians did this with quibbling over common practices, like clean and unclean foods. Later Christians also did this during Martin Luther's day with views on the role of laity and God's Word in the common tongue. In both instances, common practices superseded the faith practices of the day and inconsistencies in faith understandings and practice abounded.

In today's digital environment, there is little room for inconsistencies in practice and belief because of the powerful role that technology plays in the shaping of young minds. Integrating digital citizenship traits and faith is essential for educators so that children leave schools and homes with a healthy understanding of the technology surrounding them. Specific biblical connections will be presented as well as strategies for integrating teaching the faith throughout the curriculum. The ideas presented are not meant to be end points; instead, they should be viewed as springboards for discussion, critical thinking, and problem-solving. Our hope is that parents and teachers will see the opportunity to integrate faith and digital citizenship as one that will bear fruit for many years to come as technology changes and faith grows. Remember that technology is a gift from God, and we are His stewards to use it faithfully and teach faithful usage to future generations.

Additional Resources

- **Common Sense, www.commonsense.org**

  Common Sense is an independent nonprofit organization dedicated to helping parents, kids, and others survive and thrive in a changing, technology-driven world. They have a separate section devoted to digital citizenship, complete with curriculum, teacher training, videos, and more.

- **Partnership for 21st Century Learning, www.p21.org**

  Partnership for 21st Century Learning provides a framework that combines skills and knowledge, including information on citizenship, for students to succeed in the twenty-first century. There are excellent resources on their website that provide guidance for organizing your classroom and curriculum around such a framework.

- **youthESource, www.youthesource.com**

  This excellent website provides a wealth of Jesus-centered resources for working with youth. These resources include games, Bible studies, devotions, discussion guides, retreat ideas, parent connection articles, worship resources, and more.

- ***Digital Citizenship in Schools**, 3rd edition, by Mark Ribble*

  Ribble's book provides a brief history of how the idea of digital citizenship began as well as activities and lessons for schools to use in creating digital citizenship programs.

Lesson Plans

Digital citizenship has been defined with nine traits; however, the nine areas of digital citizenship can be taught in a wide variety of ways. This book includes one lesson plan and one catechism discussion guide for each trait. These plans and guides will not be able to fully cover each topic, but they can serve as jumping-off points for further inquiry and conversation for both you and your class.

The lesson plans are intended for use in a Christian school and are adaptable for any grade level. The catechism guides are written for discussion groups within catechism classes and based as a Socratic seminar for robust discussion. These lessons are intended for sixth- through eighth-grade students and can be used at any point in the catechism curriculum at any church by a pastor or layperson.

Each lesson is designed using the Understanding by Design framework. Essential questions are meant to provide multiple access points for content inquiry and can be used at any grade level with moderate changes in language and/or activities for age-appropriate vocabulary. The standards, or goals, are ways to see the broader connection to local, state, or national standards. The assessment and lesson sections are, again, meant to be a jumping-off point. These areas should be differentiated for your individual classroom and student needs. The lessons are designed to take several class periods but can be tailored to any time frame.

Student Voices

We felt it was important to hear from the people whom we hope this book will ultimately affect the most: students. We asked students for their thoughts on the biblical principles related to the digital citizenship traits. At the beginning of each chapter, there is a student voice section taken from these conversations. We find it encouraging and insightful to hear perspectives on these matters from the very people we are trying to guide and teach—even as we ourselves try to navigate this digital world with humility.

> "We should be thankful for all the blessings God has given us."

DIGITAL ACCESS

"To me, digital access is about having control in the digital world because we have the ability to get online and somewhat control what we do online. Homeless people and those from third-world countries might not have this control because they do not have access. Since other people do not have access, we should be using it in the proper way. We should be responsible and nice to all because others are not given the same opportunity as us. In this way, we are a bit spoiled. We often worry about what our friends or others post online while other people worry about what they are going to eat. In this way, digital access is a privilege, and we should not abuse it. We should be thankful for what we have and all the blessings God has given us."

QUESTIONS TO CONSIDER

1. What is the digital access in your home, school, and/or church? Is it open and free to everyone? Why or why not?

2. What does an open and free digital realm mean for users? What are some privileges? responsibilities? dangers?

3. What kind of digital access do we think is appropriate for children and young adults? Why?

THROUGH THE CENTURIES and across the oceans, people have been isolated. Isolation was a relatively normal part of life for much of human history. Physical distance was a barrier that was little conquered except by armies or empires. When God called Abram to leave his home in Ur, it would have been thought of as a completely insane plan. There was no famine in the land or foreign invader forcing them to leave. Isolation meant peace and security from attackers, and walled cities ensured isolation and safety.

The normalcy of isolation can also be seen in Jesus' interaction with the woman at the well (John 4:1–42). Jews were to isolate themselves from Samaritans. In the Jewish mind-set, Gentiles had no place within their society. Jesus brought that barrier down when He engaged the woman at the well and offered her salvation. She had direct access to the Father through the Son.

Despite the freedom that Jesus brought, personal and cultural isolation continued for many centuries. Technologies like Roman roads and aqueducts, Gutenberg's printing press, nautical exploration across the Atlantic Ocean, and the telegraph all lessened isolation and provided people with greater access to the wonders of the world. Although it may not seem like we are in such a momentous time in history as these, certainly we are and even more. Modern technologies and the digital access they provide shrink the world in a theoretical sense, but they also nearly eliminate isolation completely and open up access like never before.

Digital access can be defined as "creating an environment for everyone to have equal rights and access to technology." In a broader sense, digital access eliminates the space between people, events, and things. It brings people closer together even when they are physically separated. While the concept of digital access may seem like rose-colored glass, there are many areas that need to be carefully debated, thoughtfully planned, and strategically implemented to provide digital access with equity while keeping institutions and individuals safe.

Digital Rights

As individuals of our global world, what exactly are our rights? What are our privileges? And what are our responsibilities? As citizens of the United States, we have rights. These are outlined in the US Constitution. These are the guarantees we have for life within our borders. Our privileges could be thought of as the US legal code. We have the privilege of doing many, many things as long as they fall within the parameters of what is legal. As long as we are not doing anything illegal, we have the privilege to do whatever we want! Our responsibilities are somewhat different though. There are no laws dictating how to act responsibly—no amendment to the Constitution telling us how to treat others. Our responsibilities are a matter of ethical and moral character and can be different for different people. Making decisions about our digital rights falls within the realm of this three-faced paradigm.

Digital rights are not easy to identify or conceptualize without thinking in a holistic way. Rights, privileges, and responsibilities are all important in today's world, but

- In our post-Christian culture, is it possible to define a difference between a right and a privilege?

- Is the debate on what is truth and who defines truth applicable for defining and deciding on digital access?

in varying ways. When a child turns thirteen, does he or she have the right to a smartphone? As parents, do we have a responsibility to provide our teenagers with smartphones? Or should digital access be an earned privilege?

Let's think about this in another way. Think about people who visit your church or school campus. Do they have a right to free Internet? Is it a privilege that they receive? (After all, you want to be accommodating to your guests!) Or does your organization have a responsibility to provide it based on your church or school's expectations? As this illustration shows, there are no easy answers to digital access. Schools and churches need to struggle through these types of questions to ensure that we are providing digital rights, in whatever shape or form your organization is comfortable with, so that our students, parents, and other community members can be successful in the digital world.

WHO HAS THE RIGHT TO DIGITAL ACCESS?

Thinking about digital rights is a start, but we must go deeper. Perhaps your organization has decided to offer an open network for members and visitors to your church and school. What groups are part of your organization? Church members, school parents, youth? Any of these are possibilities. Have you considered homeless people, those living in poverty, and the working poor in your midst? Do they have a right to use your digital network?

Many organizations have actually excluded the latter by means of turning off the free Internet access in the evening and on the weekends. Some organizations have access that is password protected or have networks that are hidden so that only those who are verified members of the community are able to access digital content—those people who are known and trusted by the organization through some sort of verification process. Whatever that process is, you are actually granting a digital right to them. Now ask yourself, is that right equitable or fair?

We can already hear the argument: "Why should someone be able to use our resources when they have not paid for them? They are not doing church or school business, so why should they be allowed on the network?" While these are valid questions to ask, the rebuttal could also be posed: "Why do you give free food to those who have not paid for it? Why do you give money to those who have not earned it?" Digital access may not seem as important as food or money, but in today's digital age, it most certainly is, as we will find out in the digital commerce chapter.

Discuss with your students the idea of rights versus responsibilities versus privileges.

Who provides rights? In the US, our central government structure provides for our rights and safeguards them. How does this translate into the life of a Christian and into a biblical worldview?

Is having the right to digital content the same as having the right to free speech or freedom of religion?

Digital Access

Debating, defining, and deciding on who has the right to digital access is no easy task, but we hope that all organizations will take a careful look at this issue because it determines who even has digital access at all. It is no secret that the federal government of the United States wants to provide digital access to everyone. Take a careful look at your phone bill, and you will see charges you are paying to provide greater digital access. While no one likes these added taxes, they certainly help us all. As more cellular towers go up, more fiber optic wires are laid, and more satellites are launched, digital access grows.

Those types of access are on a macro level. On a micro level, digital access is much more individual and localized. Individual businesses or homes decide if they will get Internet access, what the speed will be, and how it will be set up (hardwired or wireless). No matter where digital access is installed, society is pushing toward greater and expanded access to technology. The best example we can give is when we were growing up in the 1980s and 1990s and our parents had VHF/UHF television. (If you do not know what that means, you are blessed!) We also had a typewriter at home. Now I will concede that I grew up in a very simple and marvelously loving home, but we were technologically isolated. When I go to my parents' home (they live in the same home today that I grew up in), they have satellite TV and high-speed Internet with multiple computing devices in the home. Digital access is growing!

We might assume that growing digital access means the students we serve all have this updated technology. Sadly, many students, even in our Christian schools, lack access to the digital resources necessary for most school projects. As technology in schools grows, the demand for digital access at home grows as well. Online textbooks, resources, collaboration, and other special projects have created a need for students to have access to the Internet and other digital sources off school hours and property. This is a gap that needs to be bridged for students.

PROVIDING DIGITAL ACCESS

Providing digital access to church and school constituents may not be the top priority of your ministry; however, after careful consideration of what your members are being asked to do and how much you use digital content, your ministry may want to consider the implications. In a Lutheran church and school that may or may not serve large numbers of students and members, digital access is key. Many schools are asking students to be immersed in educational content online, and churches are using things like online giving, emails, and websites to communicate about almost everything. Should your members come to a digital black hole when they enter campus?

Some of you might be asking, "We have Wi-Fi, so what's the big deal?" Our question for you is this: Does everyone who comes on your campus have access to it? We have been on the campuses of some large ministries that open their Wi-Fi to any visitor. This promotes engagement with their ministry's digital material and also an edge when accessing digital content of any source. Many ministries find clever ways to give access while directing visitors to important content. One such way is requiring a guest to check in at the location on a social media site before gaining access to the church or school's guest Wi-Fi. This means that every time someone logs on to the guest network, the church and school get social media exposure! Another option is to direct the guest Wi-Fi user to the church's website automatically upon connection. Drive people to where you want them (that is, to your ministry) and provide a service that they need (which is the heart of all ministry). Digital access can directly enhance ministry!

We often hear naysayers emphasize the importance of "cyber security" or claim that "providing Internet access to those people who are not a direct part of the ministry is like giving away free things." But in the twenty-first century, providing digital access—that is, Internet access—is often part of ministry. When visitors are logged on to the free Wi-Fi your ministry provides, you still have control over what they can access safely and what is blocked. Many people in need today may not have a place to sleep at night, but they may have a smartphone. While this might sound upside down, it illustrates just how important it is for people to have digital access. What a great ministry your organization could provide to those in need by just giving them a free entry point to the digital world.

In schools, digital access is even more important. Students often need to access digital content to complete their homework. Does your school have any way for students who have limited or no Internet to use this content after school hours? Is it free? We hear many stories of students going to coffee shops, public libraries, or restaurants for this kind of access. We believe that it is much more important for students to be working in your safe school environment than at a coffee shop. Finding

THINK ABOUT IT

- How much more social media traffic could your organization drive if you provided free access to digital content?

- How much more influence could you have within your community by providing digital access?

- Would there be an extra cost by providing this for free? If not, why not offer it? If so, how can these costs be mitigated?

ways to implement and finance this may not be simple, but when you view it as an aspect of your ministry, it may be easier to make it happen.

DIGITAL ACCESS IN SCHOOLS

In the world of education, there is a substantial divide between those who have digital access and those who don't. According to the Pew Research Center, 84 percent of adults used the Internet as of 2015.[1] Those of us in education know that we must prepare children for digital access as adults, so we provide them opportunities in school. However, what about when they leave our classrooms? And how do we begin to teach the fact that not everyone has digital access, that it is a privilege not universally available?

This kind of digital divide can put students into categories of "us" versus "them." Even as teachers, we might not always give consideration to or make modifications for those students who do not have access. In fact, we may not even know which families are without access. Not having digital access has become an income stigma, and we must help to change that and educate our students about it. As educators, we must also be cognizant of the different ways we are either enabling or disabling students and families to access school resources, information, contacts, and so forth. There is something to be said for schools upgrading their services to the twenty-first century, but that should not mean leaving behind those students and families who cannot afford to do the same.

For those schools that provide digital access to their students, there is another access question to ponder: Internet filters. The Telecommunications Act of 1996 instituted the federal E-rate program for schools to discount their Internet bills from 20 to 90 percent.[2] In 1996, before the E-rate program, only 14 percent of schools had Internet access; in 2005, that number had jumped to 94 percent.[3] While this digital access trend has continued, a whopping 98 percent of schools filter online content. Is this really providing digital access? Students have even become so savvy

---

1 Perrin and Duggan, "Americans' Internet Access."

2 Federal Communications Commission (FCC), "E-Rate."

3 FCC, "Update of E-Rate."

at finding ways to work around the blockers that some have sold their blocker-evading secrets to classmates![4]

The divide in digital access is perpetuated when students have some access at school, other access on their personal devices, and still different access at home. While we do not suggest removing all content filters from your digital network, it is a critical topic to discuss. How can students learn how to appropriately access digital content without access to it? Some schools have chosen to open up access and remove blockers; others have chosen to lock down key learning tools like YouTube. Where does

Try This!

ACCESSING ACCESS

Have students keep track of their technology usage for one day. Have them log the times and types of access.

After they have a log, have students reflect on how easy or hard it was to connect. What was a barrier? What enabled them? How could that enable or limit others?

Have students brainstorm ways for them to help others gain access to digital content.

Try This!

Discuss the us versus them mentality we might have. How can we combat this stigma?

Discuss how God has created the gift of technology, yet not everyone has this gift available to them. How can we help provide appropriate access?

Not every person who lacks digital access is poor. Some rural areas still have limited access. Discuss how God does not want us to judge others based on their social status and how it is our identity in Christ that gives us value.

---

4 Paul, "School's Efforts."

your organization stand on this topic? Who has had meaningful discussions about it?

In the digitally saturated world we live in, it's easy to lose sight of what is important. Things like our personal technology devices and online gaming can consume our lives. However, God points us toward something greater. His Son, Jesus, gives us direct access to the Father. His gift of technology is something that we can all use to provide greater access not only to digital content, but also to God's eternally saving truth in His Word.

Classroom Lesson Plan
Full Electronic Participation in Society

OVERVIEW

At first glance, technology seems like it is available to everyone, but not everyone has access or the same opportunities that technology can bring. Digital access works toward equal rights and access for everyone in our society so that we might bring about greater equity of opportunities. Productivity in our world is dependent upon technology; even churches and schools depend heavily on technology. Equal access to technology makes the world smaller, brings people together, and opens the door for Christ's message to be shared freely.

BIG IDEA: **DIGITAL ACCESS**

ESSENTIAL QUESTIONS

- Is access to digital content a right?
- How is digital access granted?
- Is digital access fair, equal, or equitable?
- How can we spread the Gospel of Christ through increased digital access?

STANDARDS OR GOALS

- Think deeply about our rights, responsibilities, and privileges.

ASSESSMENT

- Reflection journal
- Video presentation
- Bible connection essay

INSTRUCTIONAL MATERIALS

- Journal or paper/digital media for journaling

- Technology for recording and editing a video
- Bible

INSTRUCTION

Stage 1

What do you have the right to do in your classroom? school? home? community? state? nation? Come up with a list of what students believe they have the right to do or have in the various categories. What are the similarities and differences? Are there any themes present? General themes of safety, security, information/knowledge, and speech should be present. Add digital access to the list, if it has not been listed yet. Have students write in their journals what they think the most important rights are and how digital access fits. Also have them think about and write down what their rights are as a redeemed child of God.

Stage 2

Have students interview others who are outside of their class about their rights and digital access. Adults, peers, or family members are all eligible. They should interview others about the questions used and generated from stage 1 of the lesson. Do other people have different opinions about what are rights? Have students report back to the class about their interviews. Students should begin talking about the difference between a right, a responsibility, and a privilege. Students should work in small groups to come up with a short video presentation about their rights, responsibilities, and privileges as related to digital access.

Stage 3

While digital access may not be a universally accepted right, we do have a responsibility to provide access to those we can in whatever way we can. Have students make comparisons between this digital access responsibility and their responsibility as Christians to share their faith with others. Students should find Bible verses that convey God's command to go out into the world to tell others about Jesus. Students can write a comparison essay about a selected Bible verse and compare digital access to access to the Gospel and God's Word.

Catechism Discussion Guide
Full Electronic Participation in Society

BIG IDEA: **DIGITAL ACCESS IN GOD'S CREATION**

ESSENTIAL QUESTIONS

- How can we increase access to God's Word through increased access to technology?

CATECHISM FOCUS

1. *First Article of the Apostles' Creed* Students will connect their understanding of how God the Father has created things for our use to how they use those created things to share the Gospel.

2. Students will think deeply about the rights, responsibilities, and privileges of using technology as Christians.

DISCUSSION POINTS

- Does everyone in the world deserve access to God's Word?

- What obstacles may prevent access to God's Word?

- What are our responsibilities as Christians to others who do not have access to God's Word?

- Since technology is created by God, how do you think God intends for technology to help spread the Gospel throughout the world?

CHECK FOR UNDERSTANDING

- Listen to students as they respond to your questions. Engage them with follow-up questions that go beyond the surface.

- Consider instituting a daily reflection journal. After class discussion, students can write a paragraph or a page about their understanding of the day's topic. Collect the journals at the end of class, and respond to your students in writing on the next page of their journals.

"Remembering to be disciplined instead of compulsive."

DIGITAL COMMERCE

"We have to be responsible when shopping online. It is important to ask permission from our parents because we need their credit card information, but we have to be careful. It is too easy to spend money because you push a simple button and that's it. It has happened to me once and my parents were upset. You also have to be careful if you stumble upon other people asking for money. It is better to give to an organization like the Red Cross than to a single person because you do not know if they are really that person. We must do our homework and check and see if the person or place really exists. As a child of God, I have to remember to think about buying the items that I really need instead of what I want all the time. I have to remember to be disciplined instead of impulsive and try to think of others when shopping online."

QUESTIONS TO CONSIDER

1. What kind of resources do we manage with digital commerce?
2. How do we practice self-control in a digital economy?
3. Where do we find our identity? Is it in our possessions or as a child of God?

LAST CHRISTMAS WHILE browsing through an online retailer, looking for gifts for my son, I stumbled across a "best buy of the day" that I did not even know I wanted to get him: magnetic blocks. I did not know these even existed, and I thought they would be the coolest toy for a one-year-old. Then, before I could even stop to ask my wife what she thought, I pushed the "buy with one click" button and they were already processing to be shipped. Normally, I have the opportunity to review a purchase before I click the final "submit order" button, but because my credit card information was already saved on the website, and my shipping address was defaulted to my home address, it was the easiest and most efficient thing in the world to buy something online with just one simple tap of a button. If that was not enough, immediately after placing my order, a list of recommendations of other similar products popped up, which essentially led me down a rabbit hole of what could have been hours and hours of sifting through products I did not know were on the market. This experience is commonplace in digital shopping, and the medium ends up dictating our behaviors whether we like it or not. While it might be quite annoying to have fifteen products appear immediately while browsing at a physical store, somehow we expect and welcome these product placements, the ease, and the convenience in an online setting.

The second digital trait in digital citizenship—commerce—highlights how the exchange of goods and services in an online setting is easier than ever before. There are numerous opportunities with digital commerce. One is having a package arrive at your door with your product in just a mere two days. Another is never having to set foot outside of your home to get any supplies you may need or want. There is also the ability to skip visiting the bank, avoid long lines at the store, and read through hundreds of reviews to make a more informed decision before purchasing. Along with the many positives, there are also problems inherent in digital commerce. Storing our credit card or bank information on websites can lead to identity theft or scams. Buying a product is a quick and simple tap of a button, and therefore anyone, including children of all ages, can spend money without realizing they are doing it. Additionally, since everything is done electronically, the concept of spending money can be a little fuzzy to those who need to see the tangible money to understand how an exchange of goods works.

For the most part, learning how digital citizenship applies to digital commerce deals specifically with how to be a safe and intelligent consumer in the digital economy, but there is also the opportunity to discuss the biblical idea of stewardship and using God's gifts for their intended purposes.

A Digital Economy

With the online digital economy booming, people are relying less and less on walking through a department store, a specialized shop, or even a grocery store to see and purchase the latest finds. While adults frequently rely on companies to put their best product forth, Don Tapscott argues that young people in particular have a different relationship with companies these days.[1] Because so many young people rely on their friends for recommendations and have the ability to contact companies directly, there is more and more opportunity for companies to tailor their products to a specific buyer and more opportunity for young people to

---

1 Tapscott, *Grown Up Digital*, 187.

be "prosumers":[2] consumers and producers. This means that young people can engage in more two-way conversation with companies, negotiate price, and shift their buying from a typical "once you consume, it's over" scenario to more of an experience approach with products. Consumerism, then, becomes an actual experience rather than a simple buying of goods. These can lead to more investment on the part of the consumer, but it also means companies have needed to step up their marketing platform to these types of buyers.

Young people under age 20 are the most marketed-to group in history.[3] This is for a variety of reasons. One is to create a sense of brand identity within young people so they are immediately able to identify the product associated with a logo or name. A second is to create brand loyalty among young people. There is a reason that certain brands are popular and even more expensive than others. Of course, companies have been doing this for a very long time. With technology, however, they have new and perhaps more effective ways to market products to consumers. As you will read later, it is no coincidence when advertisements pop up on your social media sites for products that you had been viewing earlier at an online retailer. Emails will flood your inbox alerting you to prices that have been lowered since your browsing session. There are websites that will search lowest prices for you. Young people not only have to contend with this online marketing, but they also factor in what their friends have purchased in all areas of their lives. Since the rise of the teenager,[4] young people have had tremendous spending power with adults. The digital economy, however, has brought about an unprecedented rise in young people's spending power *over* adults.

As much as we think children and young people are insulated from consumerism, it is clear and present in their lives. We have probably experienced at one point or another a child's sudden fascination and fixation with a particular toy after watching a commercial about it on TV. Commercials, magazine advertisements, and billboards are all visible remind-

---

2 Tapscott, 208.

3 MediaSmarts, "Marketing and Consumerism."

4 See, for example, Hine, "The Rise and Decline of the Teenager."

ers of our consumer society. Because they are visible, we are more able to engage in discussion and explanation with children concerning how we should think and act when confronting an advertisement. Digital technology, though, has found ways to engage young people in consumerism where it is less visible, and they may not be aware it is happening. For example, the idea of in-app purchases has at one point been fraught with controversy. In many free games, there are opportunities to purchase extra coins, new characters, additional levels, and refill "lives" without waiting. All of these features come with a price, and a simple click of the button sends the charge right to the credit card.

Try This!

WHAT APPEALS TO YOU?

Advertisements are everywhere around us. Have students keep a twenty-four- or forty-eight-hour log of advertisements around them and where they came from. For example, pay attention to TV, mobile apps, radio, billboards, or Internet searches. Then have students look at the advertisement list and try to categorize what kind of influence the advertisements were trying to assert. Did they appeal to emotions? intellect? purchase power? What kind of connections to their personal life might they see?

In-app purchases made headlines when the Federal Trade Commission ordered tech giants to refund millions of dollars when it was not always clear that money was being spent, with children unknowingly racking up large bills on their parents' credit cards.[5] The digital world is not always designed to be a safe place for consumers of all ages. As young people constantly create a consumer experience with technology, we must find ways to make them more aware of the risks of digital commerce, how to handle money in a digital setting, and how to protect themselves while doing so.

---

5 See Prigg, "Apple Ordered to Pay."

Companies now have safeguards in place to prevent unauthorized spending from young consumers, but the amount of information that can be stored on company websites tied to financial institutions is somewhat new and can be alarming. For example, when buying from third-party sellers, it is important for us, and young people in particular, to pay attention to what type of information is being asked for.[6] Do websites and companies ask for all parts of your credit card information? What about your social security number? Knowing what is and is not acceptable online when buying and selling is crucial to being informed consumers in this new setting. It is also worth noting what type of consumer information companies share with outsiders. For example, will your purchasing history be shared with others so they can market to you? What about other personal information you provided, such as your home address, phone number, or email address? Being aware of all the parts of digital commerce is just the beginning of being a responsible digital citizen.

---

6 See Ribble, *Digital Citizenship in Schools.*

Cyber Security Risks and Tips

Risks

- **Cybersquatting.** A web address that looks like a legitimate business or a web address that is similar to a legitimate one. *Example:* gooogle.com instead of google.com.

- **Identity spoofing.** Pretending to be someone else online. Creating fake social media accounts representing others.

- **Malware.** Programs that appear to be helpful, but can harm or control your computer once you click on them.

- **Phishing scams.** Scams that try to get personal information from you by offering rewards or pretending to be a bank, business, or a personal acquaintance.

Tips

- **Use a credit card or gift card.** Most credit cards have strong protections in place against identity theft. Similarly, gift cards can be used to purchase items without giving out personal information.

- **Data encryption.** During transactions, make sure your data is encrypted. This is usually represented by a padlock in the web address while purchasing items.

- **Be informed.** Spend time investigating unknown businesses or users. Look for keywords such as "like new" or "recently purchased." Check to see if your item is licensed or counterfeit. The deal may indeed be too good to be true.

- **Report fraud.** Stop others from being scammed in the future.[7]

Stopping to think about what information you have to provide also forces you to think about what you are buying before you push the button. This is particularly important with commerce. We've all heard the advice to "sleep on it" when making a big purchase, but how often do young people and children do this when they want to immediately move on to the next level in a game or are out with their friends and need the next

---

7 MediaSmarts, "Cyber Security."

gadget to fit in with everyone else? Building the capacity in young people to think before they do anything, especially before rushing to spend money, is linked to one of the fruits of the Spirit: self-control. Being thoughtful and critical consumers and sellers of digital goods and services is of huge importance in digital commerce. But that is only the first step. Digital commerce also deals with one of the most fundamental aspects of living a biblical life: stewardship.

Stewardship

The elements of digital citizenship, particularly digital commerce, cannot be separated from a discussion of stewardship. While most people associate stewardship with giving to the church in some sort of tithe, Judy Berg reminds us that "stewardship is defined as the free and joyous activity of the child of God and God's family—the church—in managing all of life and life's resources for God's purposes."[8] Stewardship is linked to monetary resources, but it encompasses all of the resources God gives to us. Because all that we have is from God, we should remember to set our sights on what is most important. Consider this passage from Titus 2:11-14:

> For the grace of God has appeared, bringing salvation for all people, training us to renounce ungodliness and worldly passions, and to live self-controlled, upright, and godly lives in the present age, waiting for our blessed hope, the appearing of the glory of our great God and Savior Jesus Christ, who gave Himself for us to redeem

THINK ABOUT IT

- Do you have personal financial information stored online? Do you know if it is secure?

- Do you have any household rules concerning online purchases? How do you determine these rules?

- What are some ways you glorify God in a digital economy?

---

8 Berg, "Stewardship for Children," 1.

us from all lawlessness and to purify for Himself a people
for His own possession who are zealous for good works.

In order to live self-controlled, upright, and godly lives, we have to understand who we are as God's creation in our vocation before we can use the resources He has provided us.[9]

To begin, our identity is wrapped up in God, not in the things that we possess. Colossians 3:11–14 points to this idea nicely:

> Here there is not Greek and Jew, circumcised and un-circumcised, barbarian, Scythian, slave, free; but Christ is all, and in all. Put on then, as God's chosen ones, holy and beloved, compassionate hearts, kindness, humility, meekness, and patience, bearing with one another and, if one has a complaint against another, forgiving each other; as the Lord has forgiven you, so you also must forgive. And above all these put on love, which binds everything together in perfect harmony.

Commerce and consumerism tend to promote a certain type of identity and worldview. But things do not define us; God does. Our identity in God reshapes our worldview to see possessions as gifts of God. As we focus less and less on possessions, we can instead devote more time to focusing on the ideas in Colossians 3:11–14—things like compassion, forgiveness, and love. When we remember that our identity is first rooted in Christ, the idea of digital commerce becomes more than just protecting ourselves from scams in online shopping or making sure we read the reviews of a product before we buy. Instead, we must examine how we use the gifts and blessings God has showered upon us for His intended purposes.

---

9 Creedon, "Stewardship for Youth," 1.

CHARACTER QUALITY

- Have students examine what makes up their character. What defines them to others? to themselves? Have students list features of their identity (e.g., physical features, athletic features, likes, dislikes, interests, and abilities).
- Take the list of character features and divide them into two categories: God-given and worldly. Ideally, we should list and think about our God-given features more than those of the world. How can we increase our focus on who we are in God's eyes?

How do we help our young people begin to think about using God's gifts to further His kingdom? They must learn to be just as deliberate with online stewardship as with cyber security when engaging in digital commerce. In addition to asking, "Is this the best product out there?" and "What type of information do I have to give to purchase this item?" we also ask, "What kind of companies do I support?" and "Are charitable giving options attached to these products and services?" While you can certainly have young people investigate where products are made and the working conditions of those who created the products, there is also something to be said for giving back to the community that is connected to digital commerce.

For example, the giant online retailer Amazon offers the option of purchasing products through their AmazonSmile program, where a small donation from every purchase you make is given to a charitable organization of your choice. Although the donation is quite small (.05 percent of the purchase), the idea behind the program should encourage some investigation to see if other online companies contribute to charity. Additionally, there are numerous websites committed to fund-raising and donating money for educational and other stewardship purposes (see sites in the sidebar on the following page). Donating to charity through our purchases or giving extra money to worthy causes are closely connected to the bigger picture of searching out God's will with digital com-

▶ CROWDFUNDING SITES

Crowdfunding takes small amounts of money from large groups of people to create products or fund new ideas or charity causes. Below are some popular and well-known sites.

www.gofundme.com
www.kickstarter.com
www.fundly.com
www.youcaring.com

▶ EDUCATION DONATION SITES

Donation sites enable you to set up projects to receive donations or look through different projects and donate money to help others. Below are some of the most popular and well-organized education donation sites.

www.donorschoose.org
www.adoptaclassroom.org
www.globalgiving.org

merce instead of what culture seems to be demanding when it comes to our time, talent, and treasures.

THROWAWAY CULTURE VS. INVESTMENT OPPORTUNITIES

With new mobile phone models coming out every six months to a year, apps updating once a month, and new gaming devices hitting the market every other Christmas, there seems to be a constant desire to have what is new and next. Although our digital devices might work perfectly fine, if they are old or outdated or we simply want to have the best and brightest, then we simply throw away or recycle without a second thought. This affects all areas of our economy, but since digital advancements are constantly occurring, the digital technology we have or want can seem quite temporary.

In our temporary and throwaway culture, where should our focus be instead? The Ninth and Tenth Commandments encourage us not to be swept up in the desire for what our neighbors have or for what is marketed to us on a daily basis. Instead, we should look for and adhere to God's gift hidden in these commandments: contentment.[10] Contentment recognizes that the good gifts from God are not in the brown packages on our doorstep or from the money we can make selling our old digital device online. Those are temporary. Instead, contentment recognizes

---

10 See Hemmer, "Grace and Every Blessing," 3.

that the true gifts of God are everlasting: forgiveness, eternal life, and salvation. By resting in these eternal gifts, the temporary and throwaway nature of society diminishes into the background, and the idea of digital commerce shifts away from buying and selling online to investment opportunities or, even better, to the idea of generosity.[11]

If the bulk of our digital commerce includes buying and selling items for ourselves, it is clear that our investment is in ourselves. While it is important to care for yourself and grow as an individual, stewardship asks us to think of giving back to God and others. This does not mean that we are off the hook if we simply buy a gift for someone else online. Instead, we should focus on what we read in Luke 6:38: "Give, and it will be given to you. Good measure, pressed down, shaken together, running over, will be put into your lap. For with the measure you use it will be measured back to you."

We should be looking to serve and enrich the lives of others in our digital commerce. Where can we invest in ministry that serves others? How can we enrich the lives of others through our digital commerce? We do not want to tell children and young adults that they cannot buy that toy or movie. But perhaps we tell them to think about whom they want to invite to play

Anthony Creedon explains that the issue of cultural pressures to spend and buy comes from seeing our possessions as ours rather than God's.[*] When we become so invested in what it takes to keep up with the culture we live in, we start to push God out of the picture. God does not want us to starve or go naked or not be able to drive from one destination to the next, and having a discussion about God's will in our lives can overrule society's pressure to maintain some sort of status in the digital economy. Because advertising is present across multiple digital platforms, it is difficult to escape the presence of digital commerce. God's will is to redirect our focus from "What do I want?" to "What does God's kingdom need?" There is also the opportunity to have discussions with children and young adults about today's "throwaway" culture and making sure we don't throw God out in the process too.

---

* Creedon, "Stewardship for Youth," 1.

---

11 See Ulrich, "Encouraging Generous Stewards," 2.

with the toy or watch the movie. This moves the conversation away from materialism and "stuff" to thinking about others and recognizing that all the blessings God gives us in our possessions are meant for more than just our individual use. Second Corinthians 9:6–8 challenges us to think beyond ourselves in a cheerful manner:

> The point is this: whoever sows sparingly will also reap sparingly, and whoever sows bountifully will also reap bountifully. Each one must give as he has decided in his heart, not reluctantly or under compulsion, for God loves a cheerful giver. And God is able to make all grace abound to you, so that having all sufficiency in all things at all times, you may abound in every good work.

Essentially, God should be present in everything we do online, even in our buying and selling of goods. We should be thinking of Him first in regard to what we should do with what He has given us.[12] God and His ministry are always our first thought when supporting the digital economy.

---

12 See Knolhoff, "The Accountable Steward," 2.

Classroom Lesson Plan

Electronic Buying and Selling of Goods

OVERVIEW

With many billions of dollars spent in ecommerce every day, technology users must be aware of the overall digital economy shift. It is easier than ever to purchase items on a digital device, but that also makes it easier for criminals to exploit the ecommerce system. There is also a plethora of inappropriate material for "free" online that is not God-pleasing or personally edifying (e.g., illegal downloads, pornography). Awareness and comfort with the digital economy is essential for today's technology users.

BIG IDEA: **DIGITAL COMMERCE**

ESSENTIAL QUESTIONS

- What is digital commerce?
- How do we practice self-control in a digital economy?
- Where do we find our identity? Is it in our possessions or as a child of God?

STANDARDS OR GOALS

- Students will consume God-pleasing online content and produce personally edifying digital content.

ASSESSMENT

- Think-Pair-Share quick reflection activity
- Blog or vlog post
- Digital advertisement

INSTRUCTIONAL MATERIALS

- Access to a blogging website
- Digital drawing program

INSTRUCTION

Stage 1

Students will think about the difference between a consumer and a producer. Discussion can be led by the teacher looking through a variety of prechosen websites that sell items online and display personally produced content (e.g., blog, school/church website, online retailer, company website). Students should examine a variety of visuals and writing to determine the difference between content meant to be consumed and content that was produced. Have them reflect on the purpose of the products or information. Have students turn to a partner and talk about the Essential Questions above and then share with the entire class.

Stage 2

The class should be divided into two groups: digital information and digital content. Each group should divide into smaller groups of three to four students that will create content that is meant to either provide information or deliver some kind of content or product. The small groups need to create a digital advertisement for their information or content that will be displayed on a class blog. The students should discuss that they are producers and are targeting a specific audience of consumers. *Note:* Older students can use the logos, pathos, ethos concepts to further discuss how they are targeting their audience.

Stage 3

Students will upload their digital advertisement with a short (paragraph) description of what it is, a rationale for why their consumers need it, and any other relevant information. Students will then check out one another's digital advertisements. The class can discuss what caught their attention, how they would decide if the information/content is appealing to them, and why.

Catechism Discussion Guide

Electronic Buying and Selling of Goods

BIG IDEA: DIGITAL COMMERCE AND STEWARDSHIP OF GOD'S RESOURCES

ESSENTIAL QUESTIONS

- Where do we find our identity? Is it in our possessions or as a child of God?

CATECHISM FOCUS

1. ***Seventh and Ninth Commandments*** Students will connect their understanding of God's plan for our lives to live honestly and be content with the things He's given us to the use of digital media and content.

2. Students will identify how to consume God-pleasing online content.

DISCUSSION POINTS

- Is downloading content without permission stealing?

- Is using someone else's work without giving them credit (citing work) stealing?

- When viewing social media, how can we avoid coveting what others have or appear to be?

- How can we give an accurate picture of who we are as children of God on social media?

- Should we use technology to give back to God (donating via online platforms)?

- What are ways of avoiding free or paid-for pornography online?

- Does technology change who we are in God's eyes?

CHECK FOR UNDERSTANDING

- For students' daily journal writing, have them choose two of the questions above that they are most interested in and write about those specifically.

- If you have enough students, pair them up and have each pair discuss one of the above questions; then have each pair share their ideas with the group, adding more input from the larger group.

"It's easier to stay in touch with everyone."

DIGITAL COMMUNICATION

"Everyone communicates on digital media nearly every day. Digital communication makes it easier to stay in touch with everyone—you do not have to write letters anymore. This is really important when you want to hang out with your friends but your parents cannot take you to hang with them. Digital communication is also helpful for our parents to keep track of us when we are out. Cyberbullying is an issue, though. For example, you can contact someone and then hang up on them as a joke. Taking and sending and posting pictures of others can be a problem. I have had an issue with other people posting photos of me. In the digital world, like the regular world, you sometimes have to go and talk to the person and tell them you are having a problem. One of the ways I deal with cyberbullying is by praying to God and asking Him to help this person stop being mean to me and to find God."

QUESTIONS TO CONSIDER

1. Stop and think for a moment about all of your social media profiles, your posts, your email signature, and your basic online presence. What do they say about you?

2. If someone from the outside looked at your search habits, what could they deduce about who you are? Would you be happy with the answer?

3. Is there something about you that does *not* show up online? Why or why not? Are you okay with that?

Thirteen-year-old Timothy has recently gotten permission from his parents to create his very own photo- and video-sharing accounts. This was after his parents said they would become followers of his photo media account and subscribe to his video channel to monitor the content, but Tim does not care. He quickly scrolls through all the photos and videos he has been saving on his phone in the last few months or so and uploads the very first ones to his different accounts. He also tells his friends at school and in the neighborhood that he has entered the world of digital social media and to be sure to become his follower and subscriber online.

Tim's photos are what you would expect from a typical thirteen-year-old. There's one of Tim and his school friends making funny faces, Tim making a three-pointer in basketball, photos of his siblings at the pool, and other everyday occurrences. But there are also photos with Tim holding a pair of twenty dollar bills and smiling, a photo of someone sticking their head in a toilet, and an interesting video of Tim's younger brother having a tantrum because Tim is taking a video of him. There is also a photo telling his followers to follow his video channel—and to post some dares in the comment section for him to do.

Scroll over to Tim's video account to watch videos of him playing tricks on his siblings, riding his bike, and doing trick shots in basketball. There are also the videos of the dares his subscribers left for him: a ding-dong ditch on his neighbor, building a paper towel fort and hiding behind it in the local convenience store, and others Tim was brave enough to videotape himself doing. Tim makes sure to update his accounts regularly to attract more followers. He also spends a lot of time checking out his friends' accounts. Tim's interactions online are just as important to him, if not more so, than his interactions face-to-face. This shift is becoming common. Digital communication is now a natural part of our lives, and the boundaries and separation between online and offline are blurred or even nonexistent. In fact, both types of communication are crucial to how we function in today's world.

Types of Digital Communication

Through these typical social media accounts, Tim, like so many young people, has entered, for good and for bad, the fray of the third element of digital citizenship: digital communication. Digital communication focuses on the different types of communication in the digital world, how one uses them, and when they are appropriate to use. Let's unpack Tim's scenario to uncover the different aspects of digital communication.

DIGITAL COMMUNICATIONS BRAINSTORM

- Have students brainstorm various ways that they communicate in the digital world. Categorize the communications in the following ways:

Social media	Handheld device (smartphone, texting, video messaging)	Computing device (laptop, tablet)

- Students should reflect about how and where they communicate. What can be gained from this comparison?

Tim first had to understand how to access a web browser, such as Internet Explorer, Safari, or Google Chrome, and know that there was a specific web address for his photo and video sharing accounts. This process comes without thinking to those of us who deal with digital communication on a daily basis. Tim differentiated between several options at his disposal for his social media creation. He could have chosen a specific online social network, such as Facebook, where members in a community share interests, ideas, photos, and the like with other registered users. Tim could have also chosen to create a blog, an online journal, or a wiki to collaboratively create and share information with others.

Instead, Tim chose two media-sharing sites where the main goal is to manage and share media in a quick and organized way that is not necessarily social in nature. In looking at Tim's situation, though, Tim intended these sites to be social, as he asked his followers to offer suggestions for his content. Young people like Tim are familiar with a variety of different digital communication. They know how to use and create with them, but they do not always understand how to use them for their intended purposes. Beyond the basic knowledge needed to access, create, and contribute to his social media accounts, Tim has also, knowingly or not, opened himself up to perhaps the most *permanent* aspect of digital communication: a digital footprint.

Take a look at the digital communication platform of your school, church, or youth group.

- Is the platform mainly a dispenser of information?
- Does the platform allow for interaction between visitors and creators of content?
- What are the primary goals in your communication with others?

Take some time to discuss and consider what changes you would make to achieve your main goals. Have students brainstorm the following elements:

- What type of individuals or groups are you hoping to communicate with and attract?
- What type of information is important to share?
- What are the best ways and methods to share this information with others?
- What types of communication platforms exist that best meet your needs? What are the pros and cons of the platforms?
- If one of your goals is more interactive communication, what kind of platform would allow for the type of interaction you desire?

Finally, take some time to redesign your content for the platform, try it out, and get feedback for constant improvement.

Digital Footprint

WHAT DOES YOUR ONLINE PROFILE LOOK LIKE?

A digital footprint is any content found about a person in cyberspace.[1] This includes any photos, videos, online profiles, email messages, and

---

1 See Grayson, *Managing Your Digital Footprint*, 4.

even text messages that a person has created. A digital footprint, though, also includes Internet search habits, cell phone communication, and even GPS locations. Remember when you allowed an app to use your location to make the app run better? It keeps track of all the locations you have been! This digital footprint, for better or worse, is also *permanent*!

What is happening to all this data that is permanently online? For the most part, digital footprints are big marketing magnets.[2] Companies save the following types of data: advertisements you clicked on, sites you visited, the time of day, tolls you've driven through, credit card purchases, photos on social media (from friends too), and more. It is no surprise that you see custom ads on your social media home page for items you just viewed at an online retailer or a degree being offered from a university whose website you browsed. While these might appear harmless, Michael Fertik and David Thompson argue that new analysis systems can take "these massive collections of data and turn them into action: denying you a loan; getting you an interview for a job that wasn't even advertised; or even turning a potential date away at the door. All of this based on your reputation—newly digitized and networked, in all kinds of dizzyingly sophisticated ways."[3] Most of us, including children and young adults, are oblivious to the data trail left behind, especially in the moment![4]

Rather than becoming panicky and scanning your search history to see if there is any incriminating evidence, or telling students to do the same, we should instead help young people learn that what they create is associated with them. School and church are a great place to help them learn this. Start by asking children and young people this: When God looks at our digital footprint, what does He find? While we may be able to point to everyday life items, such as looking at directions, gathering background information on a topic, or playing a game, would God be able to find anything in our digital footprint that indicates we are a Christian? To take it a step further, does our digital footprint reflect our sharing of the Gospel with others? The answers to these questions will be discussed

---

2 See Roesler, *Your Digital Footprint*, 15.

3 Fertik and Thompson, *Reputation Economy*, 2.

4 See Heitner, *Screenwise*, 208.

in more depth in the next section, but it is important to remember that our goal is to create the most positive and God-pleasing digital footprint we can.

We will also be judged not just on our own digital footprint but also on our friends'. How are we represented on our friends' digital media? If an outsider looks at your friends' posts to determine what kind of person you are, once again, what would he or she find? While you may have all your privacy settings in place, your friends may not. Outsiders who do not know you and have no contact with you will still be making judgments based on the digital footprint you leave behind on others' footprints.

It is a given that our information will be permanently stored online. Young people need help to create a positive digital footprint. First, they should learn how to adjust privacy settings on social media and learn not to offer too much information online in the first place. Since sharing is not going to go away, we need to help children and young people learn how to do so in a meaningful and purposeful manner. Devorah Heitner reminds us that "having kids put their work out there (when they are ready)—and having people associate them with excellent and positive work—is a great way to make a clear connection between positive con-tent and digital footprint."[5] The goal is to focus on posting and sharing as much positive information as possible. This positive information stems from our identity being rooted in Christ.

---

5 Heitner, *Screenwise*, 189.

Permission for Posting

We often think that posting pictures of our friends, family, and others without their permission is acceptable online behavior. However, because we cannot control what others do with content that is posted, pictures or information can appear virtually anywhere, including places we may not want it. As you will read in the digital etiquette chapter, to be a good digital citizen means thinking of others in a digital community. Here are some quick tips for posting content of others online:

- **Stop and think** about what you are about to post. Is this post appropriate for the general public?

- **Ask** others before you post content concerning them. Do they want others to see that picture or information?

- **Limit** the audience of the post, if necessary. Adjust your privacy settings or let only certain people see the post.

- **Consider** using nicknames for people and places. This may not link the post to someone's overall digital footprint.

BUILDING OUR DIGITAL FOOTPRINT
AND IDENTITY IN CHRIST

In looking back at the scenario from the beginning of the chapter, thirteen-year-old Tim's social media posts reflect his own identity development. He is trying out different posts to see what his peers think and to get feedback, both positive and negative. He may be searching to discover what he does and does not enjoy doing as an individual. He is generally excited to share part of his life with others in a different environment than just school or home. Tim is slowly crafting a digital footprint and identity online whether he realizes it or not. The question for parents, educators, and role models is, What do we want Tim and other young people to think about when crafting this identity?

To begin, we know that we are created in the image of God. As it says in Genesis 1:27: "So God created man in His own image, in the image of God He created him; male and female He created them." Young people can have great assurance that who they are is not a fluke, nor is who they will grow up to be. In fact, God has claimed us as His own through the work of the Holy Spirit. Romans 8:15–17 tells us this means we have a new identity moving forward:

> For you did not receive the spirit of slavery to fall back
> into fear, but you have received the Spirit of adoption as
> sons, by whom we cry, "Abba! Father!" The Spirit Himself
> bears witness with our spirit that we are children of God,
> and if children, then heirs—heirs of God and fellow heirs
> with Christ, provided we suffer with Him in order that we
> may also be glorified with Him.

This does not mean, however, that we and young people will not make mistakes, especially with digital communication. Young people will make mistakes and missteps, and as Heitner notes, "we need to teach them how to repair the damage when they have made an error. How can they ask for forgiveness? How can they get it right the next time?"[6] Part of the importance of crafting a digital footprint and living out our identity in

---

6 Heitner, *Screenwise*, 208.

Christ is recognizing when sinning does occur and what to do to rectify the situation, especially seeking forgiveness.

The best part of rooting our identity in Christ is knowing we are forgiven, so the challenge for young people is to consider how to approach digital communication with forgiveness at the forefront of their thoughts and actions. Romans 1:16 anchors us in the digital citizenship trait of communication by telling us not to be ashamed of the Gospel: "For I am not ashamed of the gospel, for it is the power of God for salvation to everyone who believes, to the Jew first and also to the Greek." What does this verse actually mean in relation to digital citizenship? First, we are called not to be ashamed of the Gospel in our lives. "Not ashamed" means we are not hesitant and instead honored to share the Good News of Christ.[7] When we create our online profile on our social media sites, we should immediately think about including that we are a Christ-follower—without hesitation! Romans 1:16 has a God-centered emphasis; all we do is to His glory.

Verse 16 also uses the word *power* to show that the Gospel is capable of doing much more than we may realize. Commenting on the Book of Romans, Michael Middendorf says that this power includes the "ability to overcome any and all such human divisions. . . . Gospel transcends culture."[8] While we may feel the need to bow to societal pressures in what we post or how we portray ourselves to others, we must remember that the Gospel is above any sort of pressure that comes from others, and transformationally so!

I remember an experience of being very closed off about sharing my faith with my friends. After years of friendship with many of them, I discovered they were Christians as well. We confronted one another on this fact, realizing that perhaps we were too afraid to share that we were Christians for fear of what others might say. Imagine how our friendships might have grown and changed if we had all admitted this from the start!

---

7 See Middendorf, *Romans 1–8*, 51.

8 Middendorf, 50.

CHURCH/SCHOOL DIGITAL FOOTPRINT

- What kind of digital footprint does your church or school have? Have students examine where your organization has an impact online. What digital platforms is your organization involved in (e.g., social media, website, video sharing)?

- Have students analyze the impact each platform has. Perhaps have students create an impact report to share with a principal, pastor, trustee, school board chair, or executive director of the organization.

Do not limit your opportunities to do this in a digital setting, especially when it is much more far-reaching than your close circle of friends! Helping young people be comfortable with faith as part of identity development and translating that into their digital footprints is crucial to help them better navigate the many ways they both consume and create content through digital communication.

THINK ABOUT IT

- How does the Gospel look to outsiders?

- How does your school or church communicate its image or brand to others?

- What do others see when looking at your digital footprint?

Passive and Active Digital Communication

There are two sides to digital communication, even if we are not aware of them. It is one thing to know how to create an online profile on social media and then upload content and start communicating with others. It is another to mindlessly scroll through your home page and see what everyone else is up to. The same goes for any media site—YouTube, news sites, Twitter. Much of this activity is passive in nature. In order to discuss digital consumption, we must first break down what digital information we are actually consuming on a daily and weekly basis.

What does the world say matters most? How does that align with what the Bible teaches? Most of the world's ideologies—what the world values—revolve around money, power, and prestige. Those with money, for example, tend to hold the power, and the only way to join them is by having more money ourselves. Similarly, our celebrity-focused culture raises those who excel in certain activities—like sports, acting, or music—as idols for others to emulate. The idea of heroes in pop culture emphasizes certain traits that do not always match up with the Bible.

We are constantly bombarded by messages, both subliminal and overt, about what is important. Online advertisements tend to focus on physical consumption: a new pair of shoes, a more luxurious car, or even an exotic vacation. The same could be said for the types of news and media we consume. We often take in these messages even if we aren't aware of what they are preaching. While we can choose how we devote our time and what we consume in the world, there are certain aspects of the world that are ever-present and consciously and subconsciously in our brains.

Balancing the ever-present aspects of the world with our biblical consumption or faith consumption may conflict with the consumption of the world. Biblical consumption takes place when we go to church, engage in Bible study, read the Bible, and dialogue with pastors and other Christians. In the larger picture of the Bible, the message points to the saving grace of Jesus Christ. What do we consume the most? Is most of our consumption related to what the world offers outside of the Bible? Or does our daily life and practice revolve around filling up with God's good gifts in what the Bible offers? Constant digital content consumption, especially of worldly content, misses the point of digital communication: the real power comes from creating content.

Try This!

To begin a discussion on how biblical principles apply to digital communication, we must first identify what we consume. Have students use the chart below to identify sources of print or digital media that they might consume on a daily basis. This might include textbooks, text messages, web pages, podcasts, radio, music, apps, and more. Once you've identified the what, fill in the actual messages being consumed.

WHAT?	MESSAGE?

After filling in the chart, discuss the following questions:

- What is the largest amount of media you consume?
- What are the primary messages or information you are consuming?
- How much of what you consume is Bible-based?
- What have you learned about your media consumption?

ACTIVE CREATION

Some people shy away from any content creation. This may be because they feel like they do not have anything valuable to say, do not have the technological knowledge/access/resources to create content, do not think anyone is paying attention, or are too afraid to share it with others. But content creation is what most children are interested in doing, both in and out of school. Young people may be putting together videos of their recent skateboarding trip to a neighbor's house or creating a slideshow of their weekend camping trip. There are even many videos of kids' playtime activities. As you can guess, not all content creation is influential or high quality, but that is where young people need help and guidance to make their creations focused, purposeful, and mindful of the type of identity they want to present and the type of digital footprint they want to leave behind. Leaving behind a legacy of positive digital content is important as it will affect their futures, even though they do not realize it now.

Our vocation shines through in our digital communication. Basically, all of us are digital communicators, so it's a part of our lives. Gene Edward Veith Jr. reminds us that "we are not doing good works for God—we are doing good works for our neighbor. This locates moral action in the real, messy world of everyday life, in the conflicts and responsibilities of the world—not in inner attitudes or abstract ideals, but in concrete interactions with other people."[9] Glorifying God with our words and actions is important, of course, but we are here to help our neighbors. What are we doing with our digital communication (both every day and in what we create) that serves others?

Remember Tim at the beginning of the chapter? While it may be amusing that he is doing dares and other activities and making videos, it can be argued that he is not engaging in productive content creation. While we do not need to take content creation to the extreme of crusades, to cast judgment on others, or to devote all our time to sharing the Gospel (although that would be refreshing), the question remains: Where is our time spent? Sure, young people need to relax, not have all their time online regulated or controlled by others, and it is always fun to get friends involved. However, it is important to spend time discussing what identity they present and what causes they are sharing and promoting with their digital communication, especially in relation to the church and school.

---

9   Veith, *God at Work*, 39.

Try This!

How is your classroom or school involved in content creation to further the mission of God? Try an assignment that uses technology and focuses on sharing the Good News of Jesus Christ with others.

Examples:

- Pack boxes for Operation Christmas Child, then track the class shoeboxes across the world.
- Allow students to use the school's social media account to show viewers a student's perspective; for example, "A Day in the Life of . . ."
- Re-create or retell a Bible story using a technology tool.
  Storyboardthat.com
  Stop-motion movie
  Google Slide movie
  Green screen video or photos (Green Screen by Do Ink app)
  Minecraft
- Allow students to volunteer on the media team in chapel or Sunday worship to learn the technology and help with video streaming the service.

Classroom Lesson Plan
Electronic Exchange of Information

OVERVIEW

Communication across the world can happen almost instantaneously, and while that is almost a completely positive experience, ease of communication has also made for more poor decisions with communication. Digital communication must have foundations of appropriate behavior guidelines. It must build people up rather than tear them down. It's also important to choose the appropriate communication medium for the content.

BIG IDEA: **DIGITAL COMMUNICATION**

ESSENTIAL QUESTIONS

- What does your online presence or footprint say about you?
- Do people's opinions of your online presence bother you? worry you?
- Is there something about yourself that does *not* show up? Why or why not? Are you okay with that?

STANDARDS OR GOALS

- Define and describe a God-pleasing online presence.

ASSESSMENT

- Online footprint review
- Online code of ethics

INSTRUCTIONAL MATERIALS

- Actual or faux online profiles for students to view
- Code of ethics shield (for lower grades) similar to a coat of arms

INSTRUCTION

Stage 1

Discuss with the students what makes them unique individuals, beginning with physical features and then moving on to traits and habits that make them who they are. What is good and bad, God-pleasing or not about them? What evidence of original sin do we see in ourselves?

Stage 2

Display or have students look up social media profiles of people other than themselves. Have several (two to four) profiles for the class to analyze. Ideally, the profiles should range from clean and appropriate to mildly inappropriate (no nudity). Students use the social media profiles to fill out a social media review form. (The review form is a basic T-chart with "God-pleasing" on one side and "Sinful nature" on the other.) Students will categorize what they see on the two sides of the review form. Younger students could draw a picture. After they have identified three to five things in both categories, they should synthesize what they found at the bottom of the online footprint review.

Stage 3

Initiate discussion about what the students saw in the social media review, but focus on the God-pleasing qualities. The students should then come up with their own code of ethics shield that displays in words and pictures how they will keep their social media profiles God-pleasing for everyone to see.

Catechism Discussion Guide
Electronic Exchange of Information

BIG IDEA: **DIGITAL COMMUNICATION**

ESSENTIAL QUESTIONS

- What does your online presence or footprint say about you?
- God has redeemed us through Jesus' life, death and resurrection; how should we respond?

CATECHISM FOCUS

1. ***Eighth and Ninth Commandments*** Students will demonstrate understanding of God's plan for their lives to honor one another's reputations and be content with the things God has given them.

2. ***Second Article of the Apostles' Creed*** Students will demonstrate an understanding of how Jesus has redeemed us and made us His children and identify ways to share that good news in a digital realm.

DISCUSSION POINTS

- Cyberbullying has become more and more prevalent. How can you honor what God says in the Eighth Commandment and honor your neighbor in the digital world?

- Can you covet online? What would a God-pleasing social media account look like in light of the Eighth and Ninth Commandments?

- What if we are being bullied (slandered or false testimony against us)? What are some things we could do to obey what God says about honoring our neighbor yet protect ourselves as well?

- As a redeemed child of God, worth more than gold or silver, how can we maintain a positive, godly image in an often negative digital world?

- Jesus died for all sinners. How can we convey this message in our digital communication?

CHECK FOR UNDERSTANDING

- After group discussion, students should respond verbally or in writing to the question, "What is a God-pleasing online presence?"

- In pairs, have students develop a fictional persona and show what their God-pleasing social media accounts would look like.

"It's important to help others navigate correctly."

DIGITAL LITERACY

"Digital literacy is online reading and writing. There are different features when reading and writing online—swiping, searching, scrolling up, hyperlinks, and so forth. I learned a lot of this by mimicking others. For example, my older brother taught me how to tap the screen after I watched him do this a bunch of times. We technically grew up with this technology and know more than our parents about how to use devices, and I feel like we teach them a lot! I spend a lot of time learning from my mistakes when trying to figure out something new and know there are certain skills I will use again and again and some mistakes I will not make again. With digital literacy, it is important to help others navigate correctly. Sometimes it is a quick and simple fix to get where you need to go, and other times you have to spend a little bit of time figuring it out."

QUESTIONS TO CONSIDER

1. What skills are necessary to make sense of what I engage with online and in other digital spaces?

2. When do I create opportunities for students to use technology and practice important digital literacy skills?

3. How do I use technology to create content that will help others and spread the Gospel of Jesus Christ?

YOU ARE HUNGRY and don't know any restaurants nearby. You argue with your friend about an answer to a trivial fact about sports, movies, or pop culture. You want to teach yourself how to play an instrument. You are looking to plan a trip out of town. You browse through some of your favorite professional sites for teaching ideas or downloads. You are being asked to put together a presentation that involves multiple ideas, viewpoints, and sources of information. These scenarios probably sound familiar to you, as they are regular occurrences for many of us.

More often than not, our first step in accomplishing the above tasks is looking at an online search engine for answers. A search engine can easily pinpoint restaurants and facts that we have forgotten or never learned. But what about the more complicated tasks that involve planning and sifting through endless amounts of information? How do we know if we've found the "right" answer? How do we go about making sense of the million-plus results a search engine may turn up? Engaging with digital technology on a regular basis means we will learn some skills that help us become digitally literate. Whether you are successful in your endeavors is another matter.

In looking through all the nine traits of digital citizenship, the trait of digital literacy provides the foundational support to make sense of the other eight traits. Without the necessary skill of being literate in a digital realm, we would not, for example, be able to decipher between what is and is not appropriate in an online forum (digital etiquette), define how technology can be used in an appropriate manner (digital rights and responsibilities), or know when we or others are engaging in unethical digital behavior (digital law).

Digital literacy requires continually growing in our knowledge and understanding of the constantly changing nature of online and digital spaces.[1] Having a working knowledge of the ins-and-outs of a social media site or a government webpage may serve you well today, but tomorrow the design, the layout, the links, online registration, and so forth may change in a moment's notice.

This constant change may be uncomfortable for many, and it is difficult to pinpoint one specific skill or set of skills with which to equip students and others to successfully engage with different forms of technology. Because of this rate of change, "learning how to learn New Literacies is more important than learning a specific literacy of reading and writing."[2] A digitally literate person, then, must focus on the learning processes and learning purposes to be successful. Zac Chase and Diana Laufenberg boil these processes and purposes down to three distinct areas: consumption, evaluation, and creation.[3]

As mentioned in the previous chapter, the bulk of our interaction within the digital realm is consumption. Our consumption consists of anything from our post on social media, looking at our friends' written posts and pictures, a website advertisement, videos embedded on websites, and so forth. Digital consumption could also be consuming our results from search engines: looking through the different results, switching between the web page results, the image results, the video results, and more. There are different skills needed to successfully navigate through all of this sometimes overwhelming consumption and, most importantly, to get the most out of our digital experience. How do we know we're con-

---

1 See Leu et al., "Teaching the New Literacies," 344.

2 Leu et al., "Teaching the New Literacies," 344.

3 Chase and Laufenberg, "Embracing the Squishiness of Digital Literacy," 537.

suming the best content for our purposes? The answer is in the next area: evaluation.

Once we have located the videos, generated search results, found a website we think is important, or opened the attachment our contact sent us concerning an important idea, what do we do next? Whether we realize it or not, we start evaluating whether any of this information is worthwhile to our intended purpose. How do we know that what we have found is 100 percent accurate? There are also numerous skills needed to make sure the evaluative process is working for your good. These skills will ultimately lend themselves to the final area of digital literacy: creation.

Creation is often the most overlooked area of digital literacy because the majority of us spend our time just consuming and evaluating information. Yet creation is one of the most powerful areas digital literacy has to offer. As mentioned in chapter 2, technology offers endless possibilities for the creation of material. These creations come in a variety of multimodal platforms that appeal to a variety of senses and reach a much wider audience than most print-based mediums. Creating digital products also requires a unique set of skills and knowledge that we must spend time teaching and exploring.

▶ FIND OUT MORE!

- For more information on the 4 Cs that all schools should be addressing (communication, collaboration, critical thinking, and creativity): www.p21.org/storage/documents/4csposter.pdf.

- For college- and career-readiness skills for students of all ages: Partnership for 21st Century Learning, www.p21.org/.

▶ FUN FACT

The majority of people spend fewer than 15 seconds on a single webpage. Website visitors spend only 2.6 seconds skimming an entire website before focusing on one section. If the majority of a webpage is text, the average user will only scroll through 60 percent of the page. But if the webpage is video- and photo-content heavy, most users will scroll through 100 percent of the page.*

---

* See Bajus, "Do People Read Your Content?"

Digital Literacy and Biblical Principles

CONSUMPTION

Stop and think for a minute about the skills needed to read a book. We need to understand basic grammar conventions. We must know how to identify the main idea and details. Perhaps reading a book requires an advanced vocabulary. These same skills are still foundational in consuming digital texts and information, but numerous scholars argue that there are certain digital-based skills we need in addition to print-based ones. These skills include understanding how to navigate online and mobile settings; basic operation of devices; managing distractions; cross-media comparison; simulation and role-playing; understanding multiple authors on a single subject; code-switching among various sources and materials; making inferences; locating and targeting sources of information; and basic identification of limitations and capabilities of media.[4]

We use these kinds of skills in our Christian faith as well. Take church, for example. What kind of skills do we use to make sense of the liturgy? Besides simply reading the words in the order of worship, we also need to know what certain terms—like *Kyrie* and *Nunc Dimittis*—mean, where to flip in the Bible or the hymnal to access the psalm of the day, and perhaps which portions of the liturgy are omitted during certain parts of the Church Year. We also benefit from being able to catch the biblical allusions used in hymns and praise songs and to understand how the Old Testament Reading on a Sunday relates to the Holy Gospel in the service. Lutheran schools have the distinct ability to teach not only biblical literacy but also digital-based skills that will benefit students' engagement with their world and the practice of their faith.

---

4 See Heitin, "How Should Reading Be Taught in the Digital Era," 9; Hobbs, *Digital and Media Literacy*, 51; Chase and Laufenberg, "Embracing the Squishiness of Digital Literacy," 536; Leu et al., "Teaching the New Literacies," 353; and Adams and Hamm, *Literacy in a Multimedia Age*, 24.

Try This!

- Have students think about all of the things they need to know to understand what is going on in church (e.g., what page in the hymnal they are on, when to sit or stand, when to sing or speak).
- Now have students brainstorm ways that they can help others understand the reasons for this. If a new student came to church with them for the first time, how would they help this friend navigate worship?
- How do we do this in the digital realm?

Another example is how teachers and students encounter a religion class or curriculum. Are we able to connect the dots across lessons to find coherence and continual Law and Gospel applications? Can our students see this as well? Certainly there are foundational skills we must know to be more at ease with the Bible and its teachings, such as knowing the order of the books of the Bible, knowing how to look up chapters and passages, discerning the three uses of the Law, and understanding the meanings behind the Ten Commandments. When we apply the digital literacy skill of thoughtful decision-making rather than a list of specific skills, we have an opportunity to teach our students the skills needed for thoughtful biblical consumption.

Let us begin with a simple digital search of different biblical translations (perhaps much faster and tidier than having a desk full of books in front of you). In addition to teaching students how to look up Bible verses digitally, we can teach the history behind why different translations and verses exist in the Bible. There is also the opportunity to compare versions side by side on the same screen, examine footnotes when appropriate, and focus on vocabulary differences and contexts. While this can be done with print media, the skills students already possess with digital literacy make the digital activity a good choice.

If you are like us and have your study Bible within arms' reach of your bed or comfy chair, looking through the Bible at a moment's notice is easy. In other contexts, we also use our trusty Bible app on our media devices for a variety of purposes. In looking at the app, we need to know how to set up reading plans, access and watch videos, share content with others, and achieve different badges based on our consumption.

Because the digital realm is so vast, with more information than we can consume or reach, we rely on decision-making. What skills should we be paying attention to in order to make good decisions? We have to start growing comfortable with the idea of moving beyond a search engine for all information and answers; deliberate and thoughtful decision-making is crucial in order to be an informed consumer. We tend to think that new generations must naturally possess the skills of good digital citizens just because they have grown up with technology and seem better able to interface with the technology. But the truth is that these decision-making skills have to be taught, especially when it comes to evaluating what we consume.

Students of any age can learn these skills, but teachers have to take the first step to differentiate and make them age appropriate. Very young students are accustomed to touch-screen devices. Have students practice finding the Internet browser on a touch-screen tablet and typing a query into a predetermined search engine. For lower elementary students, create a WebQuest of appropriate websites for them to browse and read through to find specific information. Have upper elementary students search a topic and find the "fake information" buried in the results. Middle school students can give a presentation on which three to four websites are the best sources for a certain topic; they can pick their own topics and should give evidence for why those specific websites are reliable.

In high school (or at any grade level), students can create their own websites filled with information from reputable sources to provide a resource for others. Have a class competition to see who gets the most hits and is the highest in search results. These are simple mini lessons that could be tacked on to any content lesson at any grade.

Try This!

DIGITAL SKILLS

- Navigating online and mobile settings

    Have students identify different features of a quality educational website—hyperlinks, infographics, sidebars, tabs to other content, and so forth. Make a list of the features, how they work, and what the expectations are when you use them.

    Discuss features of a web browser, such as forward and back buttons, how to right- click, and other basic navigation.

- Cross-media comparison

    Put students in groups of three and give them three different sources that contain similar information (e.g., articles, websites, or videos). Have each individual student take notes on one source, detailing the main idea, facts, opinions, and other important information. Have students compare notes and identify points of similarities and differences. Discuss why these differences exist.

- Locating and targeting sources of information

    Help students refine their keyword searches from basic to specific.

    Discuss the differences in website endings, such as .gov, .edu, .org, and .com, and the different content found in each type of source.

    View preselected websites, one strong and one weak. After viewing, discuss the strengths and weaknesses of each to guide students to look for specific information (such as author, date, sources cited) when they view websites.

    Spend time examining the nontext features of a website. What are the visuals? Do they contribute to the source information?

EVALUATION

In order to effectively evaluate sources and information, students must learn how to make inferences about the evidence presented. We want to "raise a generation of students who always question the information they read for reliability and accuracy, always read to infer bias or point of view, and always check the sources they encounter while reading."[5] Society today struggles with two different, yet alarming ideas: post-truth and fake news. The Oxford Dictionaries company selected *post-truth* as the 2016 word of the year, defining it as "relating to or denoting circumstances in which objective facts are less influential in shaping public opinion than appeals to emotion and personal belief."[6] Some people don't necessarily care that all the facts and evidence are there; they will believe what they want to believe.

The idea of post-truth presents an opportunity for us to stop and interpret what the world presents as truth by filtering it through the one truth found in the Bible. We can grow comfortable keeping biblical truths separate from the worldview we run into on a daily basis. Because appeals to emotion can easily obscure what we know to be true and what is clear in the Bible, we have to guard our hearts and minds against falling prey to such traps. Good evaluation skills are crucial to overcoming such traps. Keeping biblical truths present and in the forefront is the first piece of evaluation.

Good evaluation requires spending time to find the truth rather than ignoring it or getting only a small portion of the answer. Consider something simple, such as how a major search engine like Google arranges search results: by the frequency of keywords, by how long the webpage has existed, and most important, by the number of other webpages that link to the page.[7] This helps good and accurate content rise to the top of search results, but sometimes bad information gets linked too. We must

---

5 Leu et al., "Teaching the New Literacies," 353.

6 Oxford Dictionaries, "Word of the Year 2016."

7 See Strickland, "How Google Works."

still spend time examining information, comparing and contrasting it with other resources, and making connections.

Try This!

TEACHING EVALUATION SKILLS

- Examine prior knowledge (both print- and technology-based content and search methods).
- Have a handout like this one to help identify important points or keywords of information for students to find and review.

Three-Column Vocabulary/Key Points Explorer		
Key Vocabulary/ Key Ideas	**Three-Word Description**	**Definition**

- Read brief snippets of information to see if content is worthwhile to explore.
- Plan (set a purpose), predict (where will this choice lead?), monitor (is this good information?), and evaluate (is the content relevant?).

Having a strong foundation of evaluation skills can also combat one of the more prevalent problems in online media: fake news. While there always seems to be an upswing of fake news around important events—elections, weather-related catastrophes, terrorist attacks—fake news is not necessarily anything new. We have always had to look at whether something is a credible source or not. In the print world, this usually means that most anything published in books or magazines was deemed credible, although we all understand that most gossip publications contain false content—right?

For digital content, however, there is no guarantee that someone researched or verified the information, which is why learning evaluation skills is so important. We must become literate in the differences between website endings. For example, website endings of .org, .gov, and .edu typically represent legitimate organizations whose web content you can verify and trust. Business and individual websites that have .com endings are usually public domain, do not have to go through the same verification process as government websites, and can share information that may not be updated or accurate. On reliable websites, it should not be difficult to find authors, organizations, or even the publication year of specific pages. If it is difficult to locate this important information, the information on the website may not be credible. When evaluating online content, we should ask ourselves, our children, and our students to determine the author of the webpage, the intended audience, any missing details, and where to find credible and accurate information on the topic.[8] The goal is not just to know when we are looking at fake news, but also to know how to stop spreading it ourselves and how to prevent others from spreading it.

We must remember that the Eighth Commandment says we are not to give false testimony against our neighbor. The explanation of the Eighth Commandment in the Small Catechism says that this includes not telling lies, betraying, slandering, or otherwise hurting the reputations of others. Spreading and publishing false information online or failing to verify the information we read online may hurt God's gift of a good reputation for others. Children and young people need to be reminded to pause before they share, retweet, or repost any information of which they do not know the origin.

---

8 See Baker, "Detecting Fake News."

Recognizing False Content Online—The New 5 Ws[9]

- **WHAT kind of false content should I watch for?**

  Hoaxes, ads, scams.

- **WHY is it being spread around?**

  Is the information tied to strong emotions?

- **WHO is spreading it?**

  Is it a legitimate source?
  Is it from an expert?
  Has the source posted about this before?

- **WHEN did it start spreading?**

  Has the information been posted before?
  Is the information brand-new from a brand-new source?

- **WHERE else can I find out if something is real or fake?**

  Use the search term "hoax" with the content.
  Do a reverse search for pictures or images at www.tineye.com.
  Check out www.snopes.com, a fact-checking website.

CREATION

It is now easier than ever for a person to create and publish something online or on a digital platform. This could include a social media post, a mobile app, a picture-sharing platform, a simple webpage, or even a product to sell. Creating is exciting, yet it can be overwhelming to create content that is authentic, multimodal (appealing to multiple senses), and far-reaching.[10] Authenticity is key here in that there are vast amounts of information and graphics already on the Internet, and we must set our content apart by being original in our thoughts and not copying what is already available.

Digital content creation requires skills and knowledge different from consumption and evaluation. We need to know how a program or application functions in order for it to effectively showcase what we desire. Take

---

9 MediaSmarts, "New 5 Ws."

10 See Chase and Laufenberg, "Embracing the Squishiness of Digital Literacy," 536.

▶ DIGITAL RESOURCES FOR THE ART OF CREATING

- Flipgrid
- Seesaw
- Storyboard That
- Google Slides
- iMovie
- Minecraft
- Educreations
- Shadow Puppet Edu
- YouTube
- Explain Everything

PowerPoint, for example; it's been around long enough that many of us feel comfortable with the skills of adding animations, slide transitions, and pictures and videos. Many of us might not feel comfortable, though, with a program that asks us to create our own codes to make certain elements work. Similarly, we still may be limited in our creations with PowerPoint presentations because our understanding of the presentation software may be stagnant and underdeveloped. Essentially, because technology is constantly updating and evolving, relying on the technology we feel comfortable with is not enough.

Anything that is created will (as we discussed in the chapter on digital communication) find a permanent place on the Internet and potentially reach a more diverse and perhaps more interested audience. While this is exciting, it also creates the challenge of how to make our creation actually authentic. We must combine the areas of consumption and evaluation to ensure that what we create online is accurate, of high quality, and original—not copying what is already available. While this is empowering in one regard, as we may put more time and effort into making something of quality if we know others can access it, it ultimately requires us to consider all nine traits of digital citizenship to create an online culture in which we can meaningfully and purposefully contribute. Similarly, we need to move beyond consuming and evaluating to taking the faith the Holy Spirit has created in us and sharing that faith in a way that spreads the Gospel of Jesus Christ to others.

Creating Opportunities to Use Skills with Technology

In order to become proficient with the different skills necessary to be literate in a digital setting, students need practice. We often think that because children have grown up with technology and can navigate a device, they are able to use technology effectively and for academic purposes. This is not always the case. We need to create opportunities for students to learn and refine the skills of consumption, evaluation, and creation. None of this skill practice will happen if we do not provide ample opportunity for students in a semistructured setting. We need to be using technology in all that we teach and have students use it as well, while also providing instruction on how to achieve learning targets. We can no longer count on someone else teaching students digital literacy skills or hoping that they figure it out for themselves. We must not only find but also create opportunities in our teaching, assignments, assessments, and so forth to help students master these skills. Without it, they will not grow and be able to adapt to the ever-changing nature of digital literacy.

Try This!

Try the ASSURE lesson planning model* to ensure technology is being incorporated into lessons where and when appropriate.**

Analyze learners
State objectives
Select instructional methods, media, and materials
Utilize media and materials
Require learner participation
Evaluate and revise

* See this site for explanation of the ASSURE model: https://educationaltechnology.net/assure-instructional-design-model/.

** See Smaldino et al., *Instructional Media* for more on this topic.

ASSURE Lesson Plan Example

ANALYZE LEARNERS AND CONTEXT FOR LEARNING

Learners

The learners are sixth-grade students at a Lutheran school in a large suburban metropolitan area of Texas. There are twenty students in the class from a variety of backgrounds, but they are primarily homogeneous in academic achievement. The students mirror the surrounding ethnic character of the suburban area: twelve are Caucasian, five are Hispanic, two are Asian, and one is African-American. Two of the students are English-language learners but are near to phasing out of ESL instruction. One student recently moved from the Ukraine, but has had English as a foreign language instruction; another student comes from a home that speaks primarily Spanish. All but one of the students has been at the school for at least three years.

Context

This Lutheran school has a 1:1 iPad program that starts in the middle school (sixth grade). Students have access to iPads and technology in the earlier grades, but not at a 1:1 ratio. The students are midyear and have primarily been focusing on learning the various apps the school has provided on the iPads so far. The school requires all students to bring their own iPad, so technology is family-owned. Now that the students have been using the iPads for about half a year, the focus of the technology will turn from simply being able to use it to what responsibilities students have as technology users in the world. The school has gone over broad security and safety issues at the beginning of the year, but the focus will not be expanded to digital citizenship. The lesson is being integrated with reading (ELA) to provide a context for questioning and thinking about the issues in relation to digital citizenship. This would be the introductory lesson of several (6–8) lessons about digital citizenship, but ties in to the class having almost finished the book *Hoot* by Carl Hiaasen.

STATE OBJECTIVES

Texas Essential Knowledge and Skills

"Reading/Media Literacy. Students use comprehension skills to analyze how words, images, graphics, and sounds work together in various forms to impact meaning. Students will continue to apply earlier standards with greater depth in increasingly more complex texts. Students are expected to . . .

(A) explain messages conveyed in various forms of media;

(B) recognize how various techniques influence viewers' emotions;

(C) critique persuasive techniques (e.g., testimonials, bandwagon appeal) used in media messages; and

(D) analyze various digital media venues for levels of formality and informality."[11]

Learner Objectives for This Lesson

1. The learners will analyze the messages found in the novel *Hoot* for political, personal, or social persuasion.

2. The learners will identify what personal responsibilities each person has in a community, state, nation, and world.

3. The learners will identify the nine themes of digital citizenship.

4. The learners will analyze the connections between the nine digital citizenship themes and the persuasive messages found in *Hoot*.

SELECT METHODS, MEDIA, AND MATERIALS

The instructor will use a mixed methods instructional approach of discovery learning and direct instruction using *Hoot* by Carl Hiaasen to focus learners' thinking. Students will participate in large-group discussion, paired discussion, and collaboration. The instructor will use the classroom SmartBoard for

---

11 Texas Education Agency, "English Language Arts and Reading."

collaboration and collection of ideas. The SmartBoard will also be used for identifying the nine digital citizenship traits and comparing and contrasting them with the personal responsibilities identified. The students will all need their copies of the class novel, *Hoot*. The students will also utilize their iPads during brainstorming and collection of ideas.

UTILIZE MEDIA AND MATERIALS

- Having just finished the novel *Hoot*, the sixth-grade students will brainstorm the various messages conveyed by the author and write them on sticky notes. The class will discuss where the messages were placed and why to analyze the author's messages.

- The students will then begin a discussion (in pairs or trios) about their responsibilities in their community, nation, and world. (The connections should be similar to *Hoot*, which has a message of personal and social responsibility to the community and environment.) The teacher will use a blank screen on the SmartBoard to write the responsibilities the students came up with to list them for the class.

- On the next screen of the SmartBoard, the teacher will introduce the nine traits of digital citizenship. The teacher will lead a discussion on the nine traits and then allow the students to look up definitions of the nine traits on their iPads. The students will collaborate on their definitions and add them to the screen.

- Finally, the instructor will copy over the *Hoot* messages screen alongside the updated digital citizenship traits. The instructor will lead the students to compare and contrast the themes and messages found by the students. As a large group, the students will analyze the similarities and differences between the *Hoot* messages, their own beliefs about personal responsibilities, and the traits of digital citizenship.

REQUIRE LEARNER PARTICIPATION AND PROVIDE FEEDBACK

The sixth-grade students will brainstorm the various messages conveyed by the author and write them on sticky notes. The teacher will explain three persuasive categories: political, personal, and social. The teacher will write these on the board. Feedback on the categories and explanations will help for all learners to understand.

Next, the students will place their messages in the appropriate category of persuasion on the board.

The students will then brainstorm what their responsibilities are in the world around them. Whether it is close to home or across the ocean, students will begin to think about what they are responsible for as a member of the human race. Integrating their Christian faith will be a key part of this discussion, since Christ has given Christians certain responsibilities through His Word. The teacher will be available to provide sensitive feedback concerning questions about their personal and spiritual obligations. Be particularly careful when discussing the difference between our Christian responsibilities versus our free gift of faith, which has no requirements tied to it.

After the teacher has introduced the nine digital citizenship traits, the students will be required to use their iPads and collaborate with their neighbors to define the traits. As the students agree on definitions, the teacher will be available for feedback and questions.

Using all of the information presented and collected, the students will discuss the responsibilities we have as digital citizens of the twenty-first century and the responsibility messages in *Hoot*. Student feedback on what is a necessary responsibility and what is a desired responsibility will be critical.

EVALUATE AND REVISE THE LESSON

- Evaluation of this lesson will occur throughout the collection of ideas and definitions, as well as during the discussion times. Students may have a difficult time differentiating between their moral and civic obligations. Key connections to look for will be those related to technology and twenty-first-century learning.

- The quality and depth of the digital citizenship definitions will show how critical the students are in their thinking. This will be important for the teacher to note since more lessons will be necessary to develop their understanding of digital citizenship.

Classroom Lesson Plan

Teaching and Learning about Technology and Its Use

OVERVIEW

In the 1980s, there was a rallying cry for an America that could read, write, and do arithmetic. Today, the new mantra is creating an America that is digitally literate. Technology users of every age must know how to "read" digital content, understand the difference between accurate and false information, and use appropriate content from reliable sources. Technology users must also be able to choose which technology resources will work best for the activity. Sometimes technology is an aid and other times it is a hindrance. Twenty-first-century citizens must be able to choose what will work best.

BID IDEA: **DIGITAL LITERACY**

ESSENTIAL QUESTIONS

- How do I make sense of what I engage with online and in other digital spaces?
- I low does what I see online reveal God's plan for me?
- How is reading digital media different from reading print media?

STANDARDS OR GOALS

- Understand the difference between digital media and traditional print media.

ASSESSMENT

- Reading fluency awareness reflection
- Digital media vocabulary comparison
- Digital flipbook

INSTRUCTIONAL MATERIALS

- Vocabulary comparison chart (two-column chart with vocabulary words running down outside edge)
- Digital flipbook (or similar digital media)

INSTRUCTION

Stage 1

Students need to realize that they read digital content differently than they read print material. Let students read a portion of a standard print book. Then have the students read several sections of online material, preferably on the same topic. They should quickly realize that in digital material, we read from the top to bottom only (no page turning), we click through to get to where we want (no page turning), and we can search for topics across the web and within websites (instead of a table of contents, index, or dictionary). There is a different kind of reading required for digital reading. Students should write or record a short reflection on the various skills they use and how they use them when they read online.

Stage 2

There are many vocabulary words that students need to know in order to navigate our digital world. Use the digital media vocabulary chart to compare vocabulary from traditional print reading to digital material. Students should brainstorm the various digital vocabulary words, but here are some words to start: hyperlink, cookie, scroll, tool bar, home page, URL, HTTP, and HTTPS. Students should work together to create a description of each vocabulary word and then try to come up with a traditional print word that corresponds with the digital word in one of the columns.

Stage 3

Using an online resource, students should create a digital flipbook to illustrate some common digital reading concepts to teach to their peers. Some examples could include defining several vocabulary words, explaining how to determine if a website is legitimate, or teaching how to accomplish an online task (such as searching). Understanding digital content is essential to digital literacy, and students will be at various levels of their understanding. Students teaching one another about various parts of their digital world will help foster a common digital understanding.

Catechism Discussion Guide

Teaching and Learning about Technology and Its Use

BIG IDEA: **DIGITAL LITERACY**

ESSENTIAL QUESTIONS

- What are ways that I can be biblically literate in this digital world?
- How can I put God first in a world that is competing for my attention?
- How does what I see online reveal God's plan for me?

CATECHISM FOCUS

1. *First Commandment* Students will demonstrate their understanding of God's plan for our lives to find our security and meaning in God alone and connect that to their digital behavior.

2. *Third Commandment* Students will demonstrate their understanding of how we should seek to hear God's Word in a digital age.

3. *Third Article of the Apostles' Creed* Students will demonstrate an understanding of how God calls us to faith through the work of the Holy Spirit and how we can use our digital resources to deepen that faith.

DISCUSSION POINTS

- Memorizing Bible verses and knowing Bible stories is still an important part of our Christian faith, even when we have the Bible on an app. How can we use the technology at our fingertips to know God's Word well enough to share it with others?

- What technology is available to help us grow in our faith?

- The Holy Spirit has called us by water and His Word into faith. How do you think the Holy Spirit is using technology to call more people to faith?

- Being surrounded by technology can be distracting. How can we keep God at the center of our lives?

- Can technology become a god? How can we uphold the First Commandment in our technology use?

- Is there a way to honor the Third Commandment through technology? Should technology be used in worship services? How so? Would it break the First or Third Commandments?

- How can we use God's Word and the technology around us to navigate the vocations He has called us to?

CHECK FOR UNDERSTANDING

- This section has a lot to discuss. After a class discussion, have students identify their top three areas of concern from this list, either verbally or in their daily journal. Then have them expand on each, explaining the "why" of their choices.

"People want attention for really silly things and in the wrong places."

DIGITAL ETIQUETTE

"Digital etiquette is being polite online. You should not post inappropriate pictures or anything like that. It is important to know what is appropriate and inappropriate. One of the ways I know something is inappropriate is if there is bad language involved. I have also heard about other kids posting bad things, like posting videos of themselves or others doing dumb things. I really think people want attention for really silly things and in the wrong places, which I consider to be bad digital etiquette. I think to have good digital etiquette you should not take the Lord's name in vain. You should think before you post anything, including what you say to other people or post on their pictures or videos. I also do not follow people who cross the line. It is really easy to click "unfollow" and really important, especially knowing that once something is posted online it is there forever."

QUESTIONS TO CONSIDER

1. How do you model appropriate digital behavior to others around you?
2. How do you—or how should you—create rules for appropriate digital behavior?
3. Should digital behavior be the same at home and at school?

CHILDREN ARE TOLD multiple times over the course of many years to chew with their mouth closed. This common piece of advice is the easiest etiquette lesson to keep, but it's often broken. As children grow from toddlers to preschool to elementary age, they are not only told to chew with their mouth closed but also given a myriad of other suggestions in regard to cultural etiquette. Sit up straight. Use a napkin. Do not burp at the table. As children grow into adolescents, the etiquette lessons become more complicated. Children learn to hold doors for others, share in chores, and treat one another with respect. Children also have to deal with different etiquette rules in a variety of situations and contexts. While it might be okay to speak with a loud voice at home, that is not always the case in a classroom. Rules, contexts, and situations all must be taken into consideration for learning etiquette, and the same applies to learning digital etiquette.

In our age of technology-filled relationships, digital etiquette is more than acts of kindness; it means following responsible guidelines for the ever-changing digital world. Even though digital content changes often, we would still consider it rude to attack someone online for their opinions or cyberstalk an individual. Just as holding a door for someone has not gone out of style, fully respecting others online must also remain the norm.

Digital Expectations and Respect

Etiquette has its roots in the Law of God written on our hearts: "For this is the covenant that I will make with the house of Israel after those days, declares the LORD: I will put My law within them, and I will write it on their hearts. And I will be their God, and they shall be My people" (Jeremiah 31:33). The Law of the Lord dictates standards for behavior. When God gave the Ten Commandments to the people of Israel, He outlined relationship expectations between Israel and Himself. He also outlined the way people should treat one another. Jesus reiterated this when He said, "You shall love the Lord your God with all your heart and with all your soul and with all your strength and with all your mind, and your neighbor as yourself" (Luke 10:27).

Guidelines for digital etiquette stem from the established relationship we have with God. Translating the guidelines into the current technology-filled culture is not always easy. Behavioral themes of bullying, anxiety, and depression are common in schools today. The Law alone cannot dictate our digital (or any other kind of) etiquette. We need the Gospel as well! The Gospel forgives our failures and gives us the power to live as God has called us to live.

THINK ABOUT IT

- How does your church or school express its guidelines for appropriate digital conduct?

- How do you express your expectations for appropriate digital conduct?

Etiquette is based on the mutual respect people have for one another. Similar to a relationship of respect between two friends, colleagues, or spouses, students must learn etiquette that is mutually respectful. This mutually respectful behavior—based in Law and Gospel, or boundaries and love—lays the foundation for appropriate conduct in digital contexts. Whether someone is sharing a photo on a social media platform or commenting on another person's post, appropriate conduct is expected.

RULES AND POLICIES

The easiest way to tell someone what is appropriate behavior and what is not is through standard rules and policies. In a classroom, the teacher is typically the central source and enforcer of rules. How students will ask questions, obtain permission to use the restroom, and hand in paperwork are just a few of the many classroom rules that a teacher must create to maintain order in the classroom. Schoolwide policies are no different. Schools have a wide variety of policies, procedures, and equipment in place to try to make sure students have appropriate conduct. As any teacher knows, a rule or policy is only as good as the person charged with enforcing it, and students will always find a way around the rules.

Most schools use a firewall to help students learn appropriate online conduct. While firewalls are a necessary instrument to keep students safe, they are not a substitute for explicitly teaching appropriate conduct in the digital community. If you grew up in the 1980s or earlier, the Internet was not there to look up inappropriate information; however, students used dictionaries, encyclopedias, and other print material to find out about taboo topics. Today, firewalls and parental controls can help block students from accessing information on those same taboo topics, but personal devices working off of data plans, spam social media accounts, and direct messaging allow that information to reach students regardless of any digital protections.

When it comes to crafting digital etiquette guidelines for appropriate student conduct, we need to look at using student input to make measurable gains to increase digital etiquette. Research has shown that when students have choice

▶ **COLLABORATIVE APPROACHES TO DIGITAL ETIQUETTE FOR TEACHERS AND STUDENTS**

Develop rules for where and when to use digital devices.

Teach common language for digital usage (e.g., log in, app, close out, shut down).

Create class rules together that include how to treat others on and offline.

Create consequences together for when someone breaks the rules about how to treat others on and offline.

Role-play positive and negative situations about digital encounters with friends.

and input in important decision-making in the school, their buy-in increases and students will be more active and empowered in the learning process. Increased buy-in and participation from students is important in teaching digital etiquette.[1] If teacher and student do not both understand who and what is important, it is difficult to cultivate a Law-and-Gospel perspective on technology use and a mutually respectful relationship.

THINK ABOUT IT

- What ways do you build time into your day/week/year to collaborate with students?
- How much of a say do students have in your school? What about the children in your family?

STUDENT-CENTERED ETIQUETTE

There are many ways to encourage student input and choice when beginning digital etiquette discussions. Discussing good use of technology is appropriate at any age. Preschool children can talk about how much they should use technology, or "screen time." Early elementary children can begin thinking about what information is useful and how to access that information in a safe way. Middle school and high school students can collaborate on how to use information to create new knowledge and solve problems; they can engage in the creative process to develop original digital creations that are meaningful and purposeful for others to use and access.

---

1 See Yannuzzi and Martin, "Voice, Identity," 710.

Try This!

Technology discussions are necessary with children beginning at a very young age. The following guidelines may help frame discussions with your students. Each age group also can make use of what is applicable from the categories from younger age groups.

EARLY CHILDHOOD

- **Screen Time.** What is it? How much is healthy?
- **The Internet or Online.** What does it mean to be online? How is it good and bad? Who keeps us safe online?
- **Swipe and Click.** Always ask a parent/guardian or teacher if it is okay to swipe or click something that looks new or unusual (e.g., in-app purchases).
- **Pictures.** Who has permission to take pictures of you? What kind of pictures are appropriate?

EARLY ELEMENTARY

- **Devices.** How, when, and where is it appropriate to use various devices? How do I seek permission to use someone else's device?
- **Play.** Discuss the importance of play versus being online. How can we stay active?
- **Information.** How do I know the difference between true and fake information?
- **Sharing.** How can I share my creations in a safe way?

INTERMEDIATE ELEMENTARY

- **Ownership.** How do I know if I am ready for a device of my own? How do I take responsibility for my personal device safety and security?
- **Apps/Games.** How can I choose the best and most appropriate apps and games for my age and needs or wants?

Try This!

INTERMEDIATE ELEMENTARY, CONTINUED

- **God.** How do I please God in my actions in the digital world?
- **Sin-Filled World.** How can I remain safe with so much sinful material online?
- **Resources.** Whom can I go to when I need help?

MIDDLE AND HIGH SCHOOL

- **Identity.** How can I remain true to my identity as a child of God?
- **Adults.** What adults can I trust with my information? How are adults there to help me?
- **Bullying.** How can I avoid getting bullied and being a bully online?
- **Relationships.** What are appropriate relationship boundaries online? Who can help me navigate this?
- **God's Word.** How can I keep God's truth close to my heart at all times, especially in digital temptations?

Online Etiquette

Thus far, we have heard a lot about etiquette as it relates to personal interactions in a digital environment. While technology usage in a school building has etiquette built into the curriculum or school culture, students must also learn how to use technology in an appropriate way when they leave the classroom. Often, students know the rules and policies that govern digital etiquette while they are on school grounds, but they may think a different set of rules apply when the school day ends.

When the final bell of the day rings, students stream out of school, and the first thing they reach for is their phone. They are texting, calling, direct messaging, posting. They are checking activity and feeds. They are seeing where their friends are and where they will be later. All of this activity cannot be legislated by school rules or policies. Does that mean the school's desire to cultivate Law/Gospel discernment in the next generation of digital citizens is only concerned with the school day? Certainly not!

ETIQUETTE IN CHRISTIAN FAITH

Christian faith is a pillar of Lutheran education. Students in Lutheran schools not only live lives that proclaim the Good News; they also learn daily about their Christian faith in their schools, families, and churches. In a Lutheran school, teachers and students have a specific class period dedicated to studying their Christian faith and God's Word. That class period provides a wonderful environment in which to teach digital etiquette. Some simple questions relating to digital etiquette can be easily woven into any Bible lesson:

- What does God's Law say about honoring Him?
- What does God's Law say about treating others?
- How does Jesus' Gospel message give us confidence to be strong against negative and hurtful comments?
- How does our true identity as a child of God give us power to ignore negative influences from others?

Rather than shying away from talking about digital etiquette in Bible study, confirmation class, or other Christian faith teaching settings, take the opportunity to engage young people in questions that deepen both their understanding of appropriate digital behavior and also their Christian faith.

Teaching Christian faith is not an activity that should be left only to Christian schools or formal church teachings. Teaching in the family is an integral part of a child's life. In the Small Catechism, Martin Luther explained that the catechism is what "the head of the family should teach . . . in a simple way to his household." Mothers and fathers have many opportunities to teach about digital etiquette in the context of a Christian faith and family life. During family prayers, devotions, mealtimes, or bedtime prayers, take advantage of the moment and engage your children about their online conduct. Here are some starter questions for families:

- What kinds of things did you see online today? Is there anything that made you feel uncomfortable?
- What are your friends posting about? Are they displaying that they are a Christian by their words?
- When I look at your phone, I see a lot of pictures you have taken. What have you been up to?
- How would you talk to your classmate about what you saw him or her post online?
- Can we pray for your friends who are having troubles?

In all things, families can be some of the most influential people in the lives of young people. When technology is involved in their lives, it is even more important that parents and guardians take an active role in nurturing their faith and online behavior.

ETIQUETTE IN CONTENT AREAS

Etiquette can easily be included in various content areas throughout the school day. Digital etiquette begins with in-person etiquette. Literature is a great way to introduce students to etiquette. Whether it is the classics, science fiction, or dystopian literature, readers encounter good etiquette, bad manners, and everything in between among the characters of a book. In literature, the characters also have many motives for how they act toward one another. This is true in real life as well and even more so in the digital realm. Why do some people say bad things to others? What is driving their actions? Bringing those hypothetical situations into a conversation with the students could reveal some real-life situations in which students could benefit from better etiquette with their peers.

History provides many examples of when people worked together or came into conflict. Using the common phrase "learn from the past," we can truly use our history to make the present and future better. Various political and social conflicts throughout human history could be used to illustrate the importance of etiquette, forgiveness, and reconciliation. These are all things that tend to be neglected in online behavior because it seems anonymous. Connecting history with digital etiquette can spark great conversations that might influence a student's online behavior.

Science and psychology content areas can also offer insight into digital behavior, such as neurochemical release caused by social media,[2] anxiety caused by cyberbullying, and narcissistic behavior. All of these behaviors have scientific roots and can be relevant during science instruction. The biological components that tend to drive our behavior (both online and in person) are important factors when considering etiquette.

EDUCATING THE FAMILY ABOUT DIGITAL ETIQUETTE

As with any behavior, educating about etiquette begins in the home. Schools must find ways to partner with families to teach the importance of appropriate digital behavior. Children learn from watching, and many students have learned poor online etiquette because parents have poor online etiquette. Actions as simple as signing an email, including a greeting in an email, and using correct spelling and grammar are often neglected today. Worse, we all know that people can get upset and angry over digital media more easily because the content may be misunderstood and the person they are angry with is not in front of them to explain matters or have a conversation. That anger spills into poor decision-making in regard to hateful language and disparaging remarks in various digital contexts.

The first lesson for parents is that all activity their children see them doing on electronic devices may be copied or mimicked in some way. Simple etiquette, such as putting devices away at dinner time, is hard to enforce when parents are not leading the way in modeling this habit. Also, parents who might use their phones while driving or prefer to give attention to their device rather than to people in front of them set a poor example for the children watching.

---

2 See Ramasubbu, "Social Media Addiction."

Second, families should engage in digital etiquette as a family. Discussions about etiquette and concrete ways to develop etiquette should be done as a family to achieve similar expectations and outcomes. One easy way to start this is to have a family night, perhaps starting in middle school, where students come with their parents to talk about digital media issues.

Have your church or school consider a parent information night for families to discuss online behavior. Here are some parent night resources for consideration:

- www.commonsensemedia.org/
- www.focusonthefamily.com/parenting/kids-and-technology
- www.ptotoday.com/sfn#internet-safety-night
- www.operationsaveamerica.org/biblical-guidelines-for-social-media/

Schools must be willing to take the lead when it comes to educating families. While the teachers are teaching about digital citizenship in the classroom, school administration needs to find relevant information to share with families to reinforce appropriate digital behavior at home. Regular communication about hot topics or cultural issues should be shared through newsletters and other communications. Schools that are proactive about this pave the way for families to have strong digital etiquette.

In all things, we must remember that digital etiquette begins with respect for God and for others around us. Jesus said, "Love the Lord your God with all your heart and with all your soul and with all your mind and with all your strength.' . . . 'Love your neighbor as yourself.' There is no other commandment greater than these" (Mark 12:30–31). This type of worldview will lay the groundwork for further thinking about appropriate digital etiquette and how to increase positive and affirming online interactions.

THINK ABOUT IT

- How does your school or church handle viral YouTube phenomena that sexualize adolescents or are contrary to our beliefs? Are parents informed or given guidance?

- What guidance do students or parents need when major and troubling news stories are sensationalized?

- What does your church or school communicate in regard to the culture's changing sexual norms? Are there any policies for how to handle these issues?

Classroom Lesson Plan

Standards of Conduct in the Digital World

OVERVIEW

In the digital world today, it is easy to be rude, say inappropriate things, and appear to be outside of God's design for relationships because technology has made the world less formal. All technology users must realize that there are written and unwritten rules for etiquette and how to treat others and yourself with respect and dignity. Working together, digital citizens should come up with standards for appropriate behaviors that are God-pleasing and build others up.

BIG IDEA: **DIGITAL ETIQUETTE**

ESSENTIAL QUESTIONS

- How do you model appropriate digital behavior to others around you?
- How do you or should you create rules for appropriate digital behavior?
- Should digital behavior be the same at home as at school?

STANDARDS OR GOALS

- Identify how, as a child of God, we have power to ignore negative influence from others.

ASSESSMENT

- Classroom rules draft
- Video presentation on online etiquette
- Parent/guardian letter

INSTRUCTIONAL MATERIALS

- Poster board

- Video recording and editing equipment
- Word-processing program

INSTRUCTION

Stage 1
Teacher-led discussion about modeling appropriate behavior should lead into a discussion about how we behave online as well as in person. The discussion should revolve around what appropriate behavior is and how we can maintain our Christian identity in all areas of our life. The discussion will cumulate in the class drafting rules for classroom behavior (digital and in person) on poster board. Students can work in small or large groups.

Stage 2
Students will finalize the classroom etiquette rules and then use them to draft and finalize a letter to their parents or guardians. The letter will be a personal testament to the students' commitment to good behavior. The parents can use the letter as a discussion point, but the students should realize that the letter represents their personal commitment to God-pleasing online behavior.

Stage 3
Since students have been looking at their personal behavior, both online and in person, now the students will focus on specific examples of etiquette online (building on what it should be like as they described in the rules and letter). Students will work in small groups to create how-to videos on using social media in positive ways. The video should directly address how to avoid negative influences online and remain true to our God-given identity as redeemed children of God.

Catechism Discussion Guide

Standards of Conduct in the Digital World

BIG IDEA: **DIGITAL ETIQUETTE**

ESSENTIAL QUESTIONS

- How do you model appropriate digital behavior to others around you?
- What rules for appropriate behavior does God set?
- How can you reflect grace and forgiveness in person and online?

CATECHISM FOCUS

1. **Fourth Commandment** (God's representatives and authority), **Fifth Commandment** (God's gift of life), and **Sixth Commandment** (God's gift of marriage) Students will demonstrate understanding of God's plan for us to live properly under His representatives and authorities and to respect life and the gift of marriage.

2. **Confession** Students will recognize their own need to confess sins of omission and commission related to their digital behavior as well as enjoy the forgiveness of those sins offered by Jesus.

DISCUSSION POINTS

- Being kind to people in person and online is equally important in today's world. What are some ways that we can model kindness and humility online?
- What are some ways that we break the Fourth Commandment online? the Fifth Commandment? the Sixth Commandment?

- How can we protect ourselves from, yet demonstrate love and forgiveness toward, those who speak poorly about us online?

- What does God's Word tell us about Confession and Absolution? How can that be applied in the digital world?

- How can we model Jesus' love, patience, and forgiveness in our online interactions?

CHECK FOR UNDERSTANDING

- Put students in groups or pairs. Have them develop a digital code of conduct. Students can share their ideas verbally or in writing.

"You have to respect God and others like in the Ten Commandments."

DIGITAL LAW

"There are a bunch of ways you could break digital law when online. For example, when using your phone, you should not prank call 911. You should not try to log into other people's accounts. This is hacking, and it is against the law. I know that there is a copyright law that you cannot copy other people's work. This is called plagiarism and piracy. You should not copy a movie or music that is online. You also need to be a certain age to be online with some things, like you need to be eighteen to use a credit card online or be at least thirteen to have a social media account. I know a lot of people younger than thirteen who have a social media account, and they are technically breaking the law. With digital law, you have to respect God and others like in the Ten Commandments. There are many illegal things you can do online, and you have to be careful to not do them yourself and not help others do them either."

QUESTIONS TO CONSIDER

1. How do laws keep us safe online and in person?

2. What are some digital laws that exist to keep us safe?

3. How does God's Law act as a curb, guide, and mirror online?

ABOUT SEVEN OR eight years ago, I decided to finally spend the money on a nice smartphone. I waited until the fourth or fifth version had come out so the company could work out the kinks and streamline the product. After months of saving and deciding on the type of phone I wanted, I finally purchased the top-of-the-line product. A few months later, of course, the company came out with a new version that was bigger and better. Suddenly my cutting-edge technology was considered old. The speed at which technology evolves is just one issue that we have to contend with on what seems a monthly basis. There are also the constant updates to software and apps, changing passwords regularly, reading through new privacy policies, and so forth. What sometimes gets lost in this constant shuffle and updating is our personal information, our security settings, and any other safeguards we might have put in place.

We have all experienced this phenomenon with technology. Technology keeps us going at a speed that is hard to maintain. Social media has us checking posts, checking in during our adventures, chatting, DMing (direct messaging), and much more. What is often astounding is that our students between the ages of eight and eighteen tend to be *speeding* around us! How do we keep up with the fast pace? How do we make sure that our children and adolescents are staying safe while speeding around on technology? Digital law is the sixth trait in digital citizenship, and it is meant to keep us safe and grounded.

Digital Living under God's Law

When God gave Moses the Ten Commandments, He did it for several reasons. The Israelites were His chosen people; they were set apart. They were to act differently because they were set apart. As Christians navigating the current digital culture, we are also set apart to be different, act different, and follow Christ's example. God's Law is a mirror that shows us our sin. Even in digital culture, there is a clear difference between right and wrong. We must know digital law, teach digital law, and abide by it.

Ever read the fine print when signing up for an online account? Whether it is an online shopping account or a social media account, the developers or merchants have a team of lawyers behind them making sure that when the consumers (you and I) use their service, their company is kept safe. That's right . . . they use the law to keep them safe. Now, who is going to keep us and our students safe?

THE MIRROR

God's Law is the mirror that shows us our sin. It is the fine print in the disclosures that is meant to keep us safe. One of the clear ways that we are to display safe and lawful behavior is through our identity. When we look in the mirror each day, we expect to see ourselves, not someone else. All too often, however, we encounter identity theft. At its worst, identity theft can destroy our credit or financial standing. But we can be impersonated on social media with forged profiles that seek to lure others into scams or other illegal behavior.

In the world of a preteen or adolescent, identity is everything. Who are you to your friends? Who are you when you're around teachers or parents? Teenagers are seeking identity, and sometimes they use the digital culture to replace their current reality. Think about this scenario: James has a social media account to connect with his middle-school friends, and his parents know about it and regularly monitor his activity. But James has a second social media account that his parents do not know about, one that is totally unchecked and where he connects with his friends in less attractive ways. This is called a spam account. They are most often used as an alternative identity. Whereas the first social media account is a decoy for parents or other adults to see that everything is going fine and morally approved, the spam account is where foul language, unsavory pictures, and bullying might occur. Another type of spam account is where a minor might create an account in the name of another adult and use that account to smear that adult's identity and reputation secretly. Often, these spam accounts are difficult to find and monitor because they use a variety of false identities and can be protected with a privacy setting. Parents and adults need to know about this and other backdoor methods adolescents are using to hide online activity.

THE CURB

Another important part of God's Law is to keep us out of trouble. The Law curbs our behavior and helps to keep us set apart from worldly desires. In our digital culture, however, it is not easy to be set apart. Young people often find that it is easier to just go along with the flow than to be countercultural and set an example using God's Law.

As teachers or caregivers of students who may be more comfortable with technology than we are, it is our responsibility to provide curbs to keep them safe while using technology. There are many laws that have been enacted to keep consumers safe while online; however, local, state, and national governments are still woefully behind the rapid changes in digital culture. No teenager today knows what Napster is. They have never heard of it. For those of us who are a little older, we know that this was one of the most important digital law landmarks of the early technology

THINK ABOUT IT

- How do you as educators monitor students' social media accounts? Should you?

- How do parents know if their child has a spam account?

- How do digital immigrants keep up with the changing uses of social media?

revolution. For those who may not know or have forgotten, Napster was an illegal music downloading service in the early 2000s. Billions of songs were illegally downloaded by Napster users.[1] Similar to movie piracy, the music was obtained in a variety of ways and then distributed to users. Even today, it is estimated that music piracy costs the music industry billions of dollars each year.[2]

No matter if it is music, movies, or homework, stealing someone else's work is illegal. For example, there are services online that will produce content-subject essays and research papers. High schools and colleges today regularly use plagiarism software to scan students' writing and detect potential plagiarism. Schools use these curbs to deter online theft and teach students about copyright issues. Here are some other types of curbs that schools could use to help students learn important digital law components:

- Use content blockers or firewalls to block websites that offer these illegal services.

- Teach how to cite others' work from an early age (fourth or fifth grade) to reinforce to children that property (intellectual or physical) belongs to an owner and can only be used when properly documented. Whether you choose the APA, MLA, or Chicago/Turabian citation style, any citation is better than none.

- Teach about copyright law.

- Follow copyright law. As a teacher, it's tempting to copy something off for the students to use, even if there is no permission given. Check your own copyright usage and find out what you can and cannot copy for personal and classroom usage.

- Encourage the creation of original material. Sites

---

1 Goldman, "Music's Lost Decade."

2 Recording Industry Association of America, "Sound Recording Piracy."

like Creative Commons (creativecommons.org) allow you to upload original material for others to legally use (with proper attribution).

- Use licensed images and provide attribution. Search for public domain images or images listed under the creative commons license.

THE GUIDE

God's Law is a guide that works in us daily to make sure we stay within the boundaries of what is moral and right. Our culture often makes it seem like whatever feels good or makes someone happy is moral and right; however, God's Law has given us very clear guidance when it comes to how to behave and treat others. Unethical behavior manifests itself in a variety of ways in today's digital culture. From online bullying with words or the sharing of inappropriate pictures, the sanctity of God's human creation is being attacked daily. Children learn from early on that they are precious, created in God's image, but they also need to learn ways to live as God's children.

Pop culture is very appealing. Popular late afternoon television programs showcase the outrageous and often immoral

THINK ABOUT IT

- Take an informal survey to see how many children ages 10 and under have seen an R-rated movie. The results will surprise you. Did you know that at most movie theaters, children of any age can see an R-rated movie if accompanied by an adult before 6:00 p.m.? After 6:00 p.m., children must be over age 6 to be admitted.*

- How many publicly shared videos are children watching? Publicly shared videos (on YouTube, for example) have no ratings.

- Have you set up age restrictions or parental controls on apps or services that contain video content? Have you talked with your students or children about why you did this?

---

* McClintock, "Kids at R-Rated Movies?"

lifestyles of celebrities. Original movies, proprietary series, or personal videos shared on video sharing services (paid and unpaid) are also hugely popular and often filled with foul language, violence, and sexuality outside of God's design. Completely shielding children from all of these venues is almost impossible, so the job of a teacher or caregiver has to be preparing them to make the right choices, guided by God's Law and following current digital laws.

Teaching about Digital Law

Teachers and parents begin teaching children about God's gift of the Law from a very young age. Although the concept of law may not always be appreciated, it does help keep life safe and within moral and ethical boundaries most of the time. There are three stages of learning about digital law that we believe are essential for students to understand, practice, and eventually live out.

First, children at a young age must understand that not everything online or on a personal computing device is appropriate for them. This is a physical learning stage. Second, children and adolescents must understand that what happens online remains forever. Every keystroke and search is recorded somewhere as metadata that could be harmful at some point in the future. This is a virtual learning stage. Third, students must internalize who they are, what they stand for, and where they are headed to make lasting good choices within God's Law. This is the envisioning learning stage.

PHYSICAL ONLINE LEARNING STAGE

All technology use begins with a physical experience. Toddlers interact with and touch a screen for the first time. They learn what a swipe is. They learn to press the home button when things do not work anymore. Learning about the constraints of the law begins when the child learns that what he or she physically sees, touches, or does is outside the boundaries of what is appropriate.

Consider this situation: A child often sees his or her parent(s) take pictures with a phone and then share those photos on social media or in a text message. The child then uses a similar device to take pictures, but of random things. He or she might even take a selfie, again mimicking an adult's behavior. This device might be linked with a photo-sharing option, and the photos the child just took are automatically uploaded to some server and may even show up on another family-shared device.

Children need to learn that their physical actions as digital citizens need to be within the laws of the cultural norms and government. This also applies to underage students who create social media accounts. Creating an account is a physical act, and many students are creating these accounts while underage. Those in authority must be committed to helping children make appropriate decisions online, which is an appropriate use of God's Law as a guide.

VIRTUAL LEARNING STAGE

Technology usage quickly progresses from physical to virtual acts. Similar to moving from the concrete-thinking stage to the abstract, graduating from physically interacting with technology to thinking about virtual consequences should be natural, but this does not always happen automatically. More sophisticated technology usage requires more knowledge about how the digital world works and how to remain safe in the confines of the given law, and students may need instruction in this.

When students begin a research project, they are usually given freedom to look up information online for their project. Whether at school or home, students have the freedom to search. This freedom may be filled with temptation to search for words or topics that are outside of the assignment. Similar to children of yesteryear looking up the definitions of bad words in a dictionary, students today can look up those same words and then get visuals, videos, and words to go with the search. The search is now virtually logged in a search-engine provider's database, ready to be used for any purpose that provider deems necessary.

Each day, we and our students are faced with the challenge of being online and having all of our activity recorded. The vast majority of our activity is probably innocuous; however, the moment we create digital activity, it becomes someone else's data to use, simply because it has been recorded. Learning about the virtual aspect of digital law makes us realize how vulnerable we are in our digital activity and how we individually are responsible for the information we provide to virtual parties. This application of digital law is like the curb. Knowing what happens with our information and how it is used should curb us from inappropriate behavior.

ENVISIONING LEARNING STAGE

Physical interaction with devices and thinking about what happens virtually with that information leads to considering how that usage and information might impact your future. This is what every law enforcement officer wants in citizens: think about the consequences before you act. Some actions online may have only temporary repercussions, such as something you just searched now showing up on your online shopping app or email inbox. However, some online actions can have long-lasting repercussions.

You have likely heard the stories of people being expelled from school or dropped from a sports roster or, worse, sent to jail for their online behavior. It is unlikely that those people were thinking about the long-lasting effects of their actions online. Our students must realize that their actions (both online and in person) are governed by laws, some civil and some eternal, and they will be held responsible for these actions at some point in time. Remember the virtual learning stage: all information put online stays online.

As early as seventh or eighth grade, students must begin to envision what they want for their futures. That future may be two years out or ten years out, but in any situation, breaking digital law could have a very real and negative effect if they neglect to envision their future. Envisioning is not a labor-intensive task. It should be fun! Parents or teachers can engage with their children in thinking specifically about their futures. If students want to be on a leadership team in high school, they should plan to have clean social media accounts and use only affirming language (online and in person). Perhaps a high school student wants to get into a specific university. They should look into what values the university holds and not only keep their social media clean, as stated above, but also try to align their online behavior with the values of that particular university. When you envision the future that God may have in store for you, you can use God's Law as a mirror to show you not only your sin, but a positive path forward.

Try This!

ENVISIONING

- Using the term *digital footprint*, have students imagine what the footprint of their doctor, pastor, or parent should be. Would they want any of these adults to have lewd comments on their public postings? Would they want their parent to be posting pictures of themselves in revealing clothing?

- Have students imagine that they are one of these adults now. Would it be any different? Would they want their children to find a lewd post or picture of them from twenty years ago online?

At any age, children and adolescents probably do not think of the Law in a positive light or see that it is in place to keep everyone safe. It is our job as teachers, pastors, parents, and others in charge of children to help them see that digital laws are in place to keep them safe now and in the future. It is vital that we teach God's Law and how it is applicable in the digital realm, as a way to curb our behavior, guide our everyday decisions, and show us our sins and the path forward. When we teach the Law in this manner, we help students learn that it is a good and perfect gift from God for our everyday lives.

Classroom Lesson Plan
Digital Accountability

OVERVIEW

Just as in the physical world, the digital world is full of sinful people who seek to harm others. In an effort to thwart this behavior, laws have been established to keep people safe with technology usage. Digital citizens need to know what the laws are that govern technology so they do not break the laws but rather follow them and educate others about them.

BIG IDEA: **DIGITAL LAW**

ESSENTIAL QUESTIONS

- What laws keep us safe online and in person?
- How does God's Law act as a curb, guide, and mirror online?

STANDARDS OR GOALS

- Think critically about laws that govern the digital world we live in.

ASSESSMENT

- List of selected laws that are digitally applicable
- Comparison of digital laws to God's Law (curb, guide, mirror)
- Reflection essay

INSTRUCTIONAL MATERIALS

- Access to digital laws
- Three-circle Venn diagram
- Word-processing program

INSTRUCTION

Stage 1

The teacher needs to provide access to laws that apply to the digital world. They can be local, state, or national laws. Organizational policies about digital usage can also be used. Students should work in small groups to identify laws that apply to digital usage. The laws should be listed and could be categorized into social media, Internet usage, or safety.

Stage 2

God's Law acts as a curb, guide, and mirror in our lives. Rules for digital behavior act in the same ways to keep everyone safe. The laws that were identified should now be compared and contrasted in the three-circle Venn diagram. Similarities could be keeping us from others who would do us harm, keeping us from self-harm, or keeping our information safe.

Stage 3

In the previous two stages, students identified the various laws that keep us safe online and how they are part of God's Law to keep us safe. Next, students will write a short reflection essay about how they will use the new information. Special focus should be placed on the digital devices that they currently use and the laws that govern those areas to keep them safe.

Catechism Discussion Guide
Digital Accountability

BIG IDEA: **DIGITAL LAW**

ESSENTIAL QUESTIONS

- How do laws keep us safe online and in person?
- How does God's Law act as a curb, guide, and mirror for our behavior online?

CATECHISM FOCUS

1. *The Ten Commandments; the Close of the Commandments* The students will connect God's plan for our lives and how we should live with how we interact in the digital realm.

2. Students will think critically about laws that govern the digital world we live in and see how they connect to God's Law as given in the Ten Commandments.

DISCUSSION POINTS

- What does God's Word say about the Law He gave us?

- We are sinful and cannot keep God's Law perfectly, but we have Jesus to cover our sins. In the physical and digital world, breaking the law has consequences. How can we make sure we follow civil (including digital) laws that God gave us to keep us safe?

- Are there long-lasting effects from breaking digital laws? moral laws/code?

- The Ten Commandments are in two categories: our relationship with God and our relationship with others. Are there similar categories in digital law that help us understand the law and how it keeps us safe (e.g., age requirements, adult consent, sharing of information, codes of conduct)?

- How do the Ten Commandments curb our bad behavior online? show us our sin? act as a guide?

- We should trust God and gladly do what He commands because He loves us. Our parents love us too! How can we trust our parents and gladly do what they tell us to keep us safe online?

CHECK FOR UNDERSTANDING

- Listen to students as they respond to your questions. Engage them with follow-up questions to help them verbalize their deeper thinking.

- Ask students to respond with both words and drawings in their daily journal. Translating their words into pictures will help them to think more deeply about the concepts and internalize them.

"We have so much when others have so little."

DIGITAL RIGHTS AND RESPONSIBILITIES

"To me, using technology and digital media is a right, a responsibility, and a privilege. It is a right because if there is an emergency, you should have the right to call someone for help. I think it is a responsibility because when you get technology, you have to take care of it. Having technology and digital media is also a privilege because we have so much when others have so little. People in third-world countries do not have the same access to the same technology that we do. One way to be responsible with this privilege is by helping others. We could start a charity to use money to bring technology to others, like those charities that donate old phones to others who may not have one."

QUESTIONS TO CONSIDER

1. What does it mean to be a member of a community? a digital community?
2. What are some rights and responsibilities in a digital community?
3. How do we create a safe digital community for ourselves and others?

Responsibilities

THE IDEA OF vocation extends into numerous areas of our lives. We may be a brother or sister and a student and a church member all at the same time. Each area of our vocation includes unique features that we must be cognizant of at all times. The different vocational roles also include membership in different communities. For example, being a brother or sister means you are part of your family and extended family community. As a student, you belong to the community of students in a classroom and to the larger student body in a single school. As a church member, you not only belong to the faith community in your congregation but also to the larger community of believers united in Christ.

Each different community contains certain expectations for its members. In a family, there is an expectation that members be respectful, supportive, and loving toward one another. A school community expects students to engage in learning and follow rules that create a positive school culture. Churches expect their community members to participate in worship, support the wider mission and ministry of the church, and participate in the Sacraments that unite them around a common set of beliefs. Some of these expectations are communicated quite clearly to members. There are usually lists of rules posted on classroom walls and referred to when problems arise. Other expectations may be communicated through the behavior of other community members. For example, participating in mission trips may not be required by a church, but the enthusiasm of others who have traveled on such trips might compel others to join.

But what do we do when community expectations are not communicated and are difficult to decipher? This often happens in the digital community. The digital citizenship trait of rights and responsibilities is designed to help children and young adults identify the specific rights and responsibilities they have as members of the digital community.

THINK ABOUT IT

Take a moment to have students identify the rights and responsibilities in the following contexts:

- Home
- Neighborhood
- Community
- Digital Community

Rights and responsibilities are two different ideas that need to be unpacked in order to understand how they function in a digital community. Digital rights will be discussed in the next section. In looking at responsibilities, we must think about both individual and group responsibilities. For example, individual digital responsibilities might include making sure that the content we post is appropriate, is not inflammatory toward others, and does not break any laws. The chapters on digital etiquette and digital law provide good insight into individual responsibilities. Other individual responsibilities might include telling an authority if you witness cyberbullying or other illicit behaviors. Group responsibilities might include having an open membership policy for others who wish to join a listserv or online topical group. Similarly, groups may choose to provide requirements for those who wish to participate in specific online groups and police any activity that is contrary to the group's mission. Essentially, individuals are bound to meet the requirements of any larger digital group they belong to, and the group is responsible for making sure individuals adhere to these requirements.

When looking at the digital community as a whole, we must start by identifying the responsibilities of participants. While this may seem overwhelming since there is the potential for numerous responsibilities, we suggest you start with the other eight digital citizenship traits to create a framework and center the discussion on connecting the responsibilities to our digital citizenship. Being a citizen does not mean we can simply sit back and enjoy the different rights that might be inherent. For example, one of the greatest rights of being a citizen of the United States is freedom of speech. While all US citizens enjoy this right, it does not mean that we can shirk our responsibility to uphold this right. We have a responsibility to respect the speech of others, make sure governments or individuals do not block or impede this right, and also be responsible citizens ourselves to not abuse this right.

The larger responsibility in digital citizenship is to uphold the rights of all digital users inherent in the eight traits. For example, we are responsible for making sure all have equal access to technology both offline and online and to stop others who may be denying others access. It is not enough to make sure we have access ourselves. As digital citizens, we should care about creating a digital society that extends rights to others. Just as teachers and students play an active role in creating a positive classroom culture that is conducive to learning, so we must be engaged and responsible citizens who create a digital community that is purposeful and meaningful for all.

As Christians, our most important responsibility in the digital community is to share our faith. Our faith does not disappear because we are in a nonchurch setting. Instead, our sincere faith in Christ should be present in all that we do. Our goal as digital citizens is to create the type of digital society where we do not participate or promote anything that is contrary to the Bible's teachings. Instead, "we should tell others about Jesus, participate in works of mercy and service, and support the ministry of the church with prayer and financial gifts" (Small Catechism, Question

215). We can learn to be responsible and even model digital citizens by focusing first on our responsibilities as Christians.

CHRISTIANS IN A DIGITAL COMMUNITY

- Have conversations with your students about how they demonstrate to others that they are Christians. Can students provide examples from their lives where they have demonstrated their faith outside of school or church?
- Brainstorm circumstances where it might be difficult but necessary to show you are a Christian, such as sporting events when others might swear or bully, high school or college parties where parents might be absent, or social media posts where someone is being cyberbullied.

Rights and Freedoms

Examining digital rights requires reviewing civics and our basic rights as found in the US Constitution and Bill of Rights. The most common right linked to digital citizenship is the First Amendment and the ability to speak our thoughts and opinions without fear of retaliation. This basic right includes different facets in a digital environment. For example, when we post something to our social media accounts or a comment section on a webpage, we anticipate that others should not vandalize our thoughts and opinions or threaten or harass us because of them. As discussed in the etiquette chapter, this is not always the case; there are ongoing news stories about large social media sites cracking

▶ **RESPONSIBILITIES AND THE CITIZENSHIP TRAITS**

Consider the different responsibilities in each of the digital citizenship traits:

Digital access
Digital commerce
Digital communication
Digital literacy
Digital etiquette
Digital law
Digital health and wellness
Digital security

down on users who harass others for various reasons. Besides large organizations acting on their responsibility to protect this freedom, we as digital citizens are expected to do the same. This means that we should work to protect the rights of others, and we must avoid misuse of the right of free speech.

Besides the ability to post without fear of retaliation, we also have ownership of what we create online—our intellectual property. This was discussed in depth in the chapter on digital law, but it is important to remember that we have the right to our intellectual property, even in the digital realm; that is, others do not have the right to steal our ideas and pass them off as their own. We spend time teaching about copyrights and citation for content we find on search engines, but we also need to discuss the idea of asking for permission. How quickly do we post a picture of our friends online without asking? What about sharing an idea or picture from something we read online and passing it off as our own? We don't often see the repercussions of these actions since the digital world is so large and it is difficult to crack down on users. It becomes more real, however, when we discover that other people are abusing this right—when we stumble upon a picture of ourselves connected to a false online identity, for example.

The freedom to enjoy rights does not mean we should abuse them. Taking time to identify when and where digital citizens have certain rights and when they abuse these rights is a great launching point for a larger discussion on civics in a digital realm. Our freedom to assembly, found in the First Amendment, also extends into the digital society, where the focus is not about getting together to play video games with our friends, but instead to take an active role in protecting the rights of digital citizenship. Unlike the political environment, where children and young adults perhaps feel as though they have no voice or power in creating or imagining something different, children and young adults do have tremendous influence in what happens online.

As we have been discussing throughout the different traits, technology consumption and creation is largely driven by the individual, and in this case, by the children and young adults who use it constantly. When

▶ RIGHTS AND THE CITIZENSHIP TRAITS

Consider the different rights in each of the digital citizenship traits.

Digital access
Digital commerce
Digital communication
Digital literacy
Digital etiquette
Digital law
Digital health and wellness
Digital security

we draw attention to how much power children and young adults have in their digital creations and how they drive what they create, post, and share, they can begin to see that they are in control of their actions online, not someone else. Returning to the trait of digital communication, there are also many opportunities to collaborate with others beyond the four walls of the classroom and even beyond the local community. The political process is tied to rules and regulations, but digital technology and media allow us to connect and collaborate more easily. It is certainly the right of children and young adults to do this, so our job is to guide them to use these rights to focus their efforts on problem-solving. Solving problems important to children and young adults clearly links rights and responsibilities together to reframe the discussion of digital citizenship from passive participation to action. In order to achieve these goals and create this type of community, we need to have clear behavior expectations with technology and digital media both in and out of the classroom.

Behavior Expectations

We take time at the beginning of the school year to discuss classroom rules, share behavioral expectations, and discuss the consequences if any of these rules or expectations are broken. Why should this be any different when using technology or being online? As you will read in the next chapter, part of the behavior expectations for technology use deal with the physical aspect. Students should respect the fragile nature of technology and know that it is not okay to slam computers down on desks or leave the computer cart a tangled mess of cords. Students should also be expected to sit appropriately at a desk when using technology so as not to cause any physical harm while using technology. Some of this is easier with a designated computer lab in the school or a spot at home, but even then, there are expectations that there will be no property damage.

There are also expectations for online behavior. Much like catching students reading a novel when they should be reading textbooks, there is an expectation that if they are supposed to visit a particular website for information, there will be no wandering to social media, email, or other websites. Similarly, if our goal as teachers is to have students work together on a collaborative project online, then everyone participates, no one deletes another's contribution, everyone leaves constructive comments on others' work, and so forth. It is easy to link some of these behaviors directly to a set of classroom rules and expectations, and we must be mindful of technology's unique features to help students become aware of specific expectations when using technology.

The goal is that adults will not have to constantly police children's behaviors. Much like in a physical classroom, where we want students to hold other students accountable, linking behavioral expectations to digital rights and responsibilities should help students with both individual and group accountability. By reviewing the traits of digital etiquette and digital law, for example, students should know how they are to behave online and check themselves in that behavior. These expectations can help a group hold one another accountable for inappropriate behavior. Digital citizenship is not about simply maintaining a digital society; rather, it is about creation. Citizens can create the type of digital society they want to participate in. If there is a part of digital or online behavior that we do not like, we can find ways to improve upon it rather than settling for anything lower than the highest expectations.

Living up to classroom expectations is not impossible for children, but they will make mistakes. Romans 3:23 says that "all have sinned and fall short of the glory of God"; none of us can stand up to the scrutiny of God's judgment. We are not capable of living the perfect life that God demands. Instead, we receive God's grace and forgiveness through His Son, Jesus Christ. God makes it clear through His Ten Commandments what He expects of us, and these apply in the digital realm too (see Try This below). We must extend His forgiveness to children when they fall short of our expectations as well. Centering our technology expectations on God's expectations will help remind students of the true motivation for our behavior as children of God, and also of the blessings when we seek out God's will and ask for His help: "I am the vine; you are the branches. Whoever abides in Me and I in him, he it is that bears much fruit, for apart from Me you can do nothing" (John 15:5). In addition to a set of classroom rules that may include a rule focused on technology usage, there should also be distinct policies to help guide students' digital behaviors, rights, and responsibilities.

DIGITAL EXPECTATIONS AND GOD'S LAW

Use this chart to help you and your students identify the digital expectation associated with each commandment. Students could work in pairs, in small groups, or as a class to brainstorm and develop guidelines for digital media use that are faithful to the Ten Commandments.

Commandment	Digital expectation
You shall have no other gods.	*(E.g., Put God before your technology use.)*
You shall not misuse the name of the LORD your God.	*(E.g., Do not use vulgar language online.)*
Remember the Sabbath day by keeping it holy.	
Honor your father and your mother.	
You shall not murder.	
You shall not commit adultery.	
You shall not steal.	
You shall not give false testimony against your neighbor.	

Commandment	Digital expectation
You shall not covet your neighbor's house.	
You shall not covet your neighbor's wife, or his manservant or maidservant, his ox or donkey, or anything that belongs to your neighbor.	

Usage Policies

Chances are your school or church already has some sort of technology policy in writing and in place. It probably reflects how students are supposed to interact with technology, procedures for when technology is broken, and maybe consequences for when a student is found in violation of the policy. This policy was most likely dictated from administration without student input. However, as students learn about their rights and responsibilities as digital citizens, they can also have a part in creating a technology policy. It can be a larger conversation that involves students rather than just rules about what they can and cannot do. This conversation should not be just reading the policy to students, but rather checking for understanding, identifying where they agree and disagree, and then revising so that students feel ownership over their rights and responsibilities as digital citizens.

Rather than dictating an acceptable use policy, schools can work with students to create a responsible use policy. This moves from a "fear-and-avoidance-based model to one that emphasizes the actions that a responsible digital citizen should take."[1] The table below shows the differences:

Acceptable Use Policy*	Responsible Use Policy
Focuses on rules and regulations.	Focuses on desired behaviors.
Rules may limit student learning and technology use.	Student responsibility is of primary concern.
Policies intended to control, restrict, or prohibit certain behaviors.	Policies developed with students with the expectation that technology will be used and is an important part of learning.
Assumes that students will naturally break the rules and will eventually lose technology privileges.	Contains clear expectations of technology use.
* Couros and Hildebrant	

[1] Couros and Hildebrant, "What Kind of (Digital) Citizen?"

It is probably a safe assumption that you are reading this book because you value technology in both your personal and professional life and believe that we must teach students how to use it effectively to prepare them for a life with technology. Therefore, we must extend grace to our students to grant them every right and responsibility they deserve as digital citizens. They will certainly make mistakes and need to learn the importance of digital law and its consequences, but as Christians, we know that God's forgiveness in Christ covers our failures. Rather than limiting young people because we are fearful of what they might do or that they're not ready, let us teach them to make the right decisions and then allow them the opportunity to follow through on that behavior. It is our job to show them the way, as well as model the importance of our rights and responsibilities as digital citizens in order to create the society we desire.

Look at your current school mission statement. Is it connected to the digital realm? What might it look like to integrate issues related to technology? Take a moment to rewrite your school mission statement to reflect this new understanding.

Classroom Lesson Plan

Freedoms Extended to Everyone in a Digital World

OVERVIEW

In the USA, we have a Constitution and a Bill of Rights that outline our basic rights and responsibilities. The technology-rich world we live in allows new opportunities to use or misuse those rights. Technology users must work together to build a global community that enables as many people as possible to benefit from the God-given gift of technology.

BIG IDEA: **DIGITAL RIGHTS AND RESPONSIBILITIES**

ESSENTIAL QUESTIONS

- What rights do you have in the digital world?
- Are all rights equal in the digital world?
- How is it everyone's responsibility to be safe and productive in the digital world?

STANDARDS OR GOALS

- Think critically about the freedom that Christians have in Christ and what that looks like in the digital world.

ASSESSMENT

- Video interview
- Create a bill of digital rights

INSTRUCTIONAL MATERIALS

- Video recording and editing materials
- Posting information online (can be video, visual, written, etc.)

INSTRUCTION

Stage 1

Students should be introduced to the Bill of Rights in the US Constitution. Those first ten amendments are foundational to the rights we have as Americans. Next, students will think about what those ten amendments look like in today's digital world. As a class, brainstorm what freedom of speech, the freedom to assemble, and the rest look like in the digital world. How are they applied differently in the digital realm than the physical one? The class should end up with a list of freedoms that we have in the digital world that mirrors our freedoms outlined in the US Bill of Rights.

Stage 2

With the list of freedoms from stage 1, students (individual or small groups) should plan to interview five to ten people about the freedoms they have online. Students should prewrite questions that focus on these topics: What freedoms do we have online? Does everyone have those same freedoms or rights? Why or why not? Can freedoms be equal online? Should they be? As Christians, do we have any additional freedoms that we are responsible for in the digital world, such as freedom to share our faith? Once students have interviewed selected people (friends, peers, parents, teachers, etc.), they should compile a short five-minute video to share with a one-minute summation of their own. These should be shared with the class.

Stage 3

Students have now done extensive thinking about rights and freedoms in our physical and digital world. The students should work in groups of five to eight people to create their own bill of digital rights. This bill of rights can be written, drawn, acted out, or presented in any other method deemed appropriate to illustrate our digital rights and responsibilities. As Christians, responsibilities should focus on how to share Christ in both words and actions; how we can use digital technology to bring people together instead of fighting and driving people apart; and how we might be safer by working together online through shared rights and responsibilities.

Catechism Discussion Guide

Freedoms Extended to Everyone in a Digital World

BIG IDEA: **DIGITAL RIGHTS AND RESPONSIBILITIES**

ESSENTIAL QUESTIONS

- What rights do you have in the digital world?
- How is it everyone's responsibility to be safe and productive in the digital world?
- What rights, responsibilities, and privileges do we have as Christians?

CATECHISM FOCUS

1. ***Second Article of the Apostles' Creed*** Students will think critically about the freedom that Christians have in Christ and what it looks like to live under Him in the digital world.

2. ***The Lord's Prayer*** Students will demonstrate an understanding of God's plan for us as His children and how we are to commend our lives to Him.

DISCUSSION POINTS

- Jesus has done it all for us! How should we respond in return? What might that look like in our technology-rich society?
- How can we use technology to let others know of the freedom we have in Christ?
- When we pray the Lord's Prayer, we pray for ourselves and our enemies. How do we handle this responsibility online?
- Because of what God has done for us through Jesus, we should hallow, or hold holy, God's name. What does this look like in a digital environment?
- Do we have a responsibility to tell others about Jesus and model His love? Is it a privilege? What does God's Word tell

us about our responsibilities and privileges as His children? How do we model that online? in person?

- We are privileged to have a loving and saving God. What privileges might we have online that could further this message?

CHECK FOR UNDERSTANDING

- After discussing these questions, have students write or speak a prayer that reflects their understanding of their digital rights and responsibilities. They may want to start by writing short bullet points and then expand it further with more prayer language.

"We also have to think of our spiritual health."

DIGITAL HEALTH AND WELLNESS

"Technology and digital media can be both unhealthy and healthy both physically and mentally. A lot of times, we spend too much time on technology and do not go outside and get fresh air. You spend too much time on the screen and then sometimes stay up late and do not get much sleep. Bullying on social media could make us stressed or depressed and also make us physically unhealthy. I do think technology and digital media can help us be healthy by maybe reaching fitness goals when you can track how much physical exercise you have done in a day. We also have to think of our spiritual health. For example, technology can be an idol where you are on it all the time and do not have time for anything else, maybe even church. Looking up bad websites or watching unhealthy things can lead us down the wrong path and break our connection to God. Technology can also help us be spiritually healthy by providing instant access to the Bible with an app on a device and by spreading the Gospel to others through our technology."

CHAPTER 8

Digital Health and Wellness

QUESTIONS TO CONSIDER

1. Are you always with your digital device? How often do you check it?

2. When you have a free moment, do you immediately turn to your digital device?

3. When do you use your digital devices? Do you use it when you are alone? when you're with someone?

IT IS DIFFICULT to think about the fact that the first computer did not fit easily in a pocket. It's hard to imagine life without a little computer in our pocket at all times! The size and power of technology has allowed for more mobility and convenience to the point that we are able to access it in almost any scenario. We are able to walk the dog while also checking sports scores or the latest headlines. Families can spend mealtimes conversing with others miles away. Emails can be answered at all times of the day (which one might think would lead to higher productivity). Essentially, it is easier than ever to have technology present in nearly all aspects of our lives.

With technology no longer being confined to designated rooms in the home or at school, we often lose track of how much time we spend with technology on a daily basis. This lack of awareness connects with the eighth trait of digital citizenship: digital health and wellness. Technology use affects us both physically and psychologically. Technology use provides some health benefits psychologically, but it can also negatively impact our physical health, especially when it's overused. Reflecting on our technology use can greatly affect our health. Technology should be seen as an important add-on, not the center of our lives. Recognizing this will help us to be more mindful in how we glorify God in our lives.

Health Benefits

Psychologically, technology provides exposure to new ideas and experiences that might otherwise be impossible.[1] For instance, students are able to go on virtual field trips around the world to see famous locations, artifacts, or people that previously time and money might have rendered difficult to accomplish. Technology's far-reaching nature shrinks the world around us; it helps us be, or at least feel, more connected to the rest of the world instead of remaining isolated or sheltered.

Technology also contributes to our health and wellness by its ability to provide good support groups in a variety of settings.[2] Technology can provide information to locate support groups physically near us or provide them in an online setting. There are more options than ever before to find others who may be dealing with issues that are similar to ours. The wealth of opportunities to find, meet, and talk with others who can support us helps to combat isolation.

Another benefit of technology is the opportunity to avoid communication breakdowns in personal and professional relationships. Because of the variety of communication avenues available in technology, we can better stay in touch with the people we care about. Going overseas? No problem, thanks to technology—there are plenty of services available to maintain contact. Don't live close to family? No problem—you can use video conferencing to allow both verbal and nonverbal communication. Businesses, professional organizations, and other professional contacts are able to reach customers and potential customers through multiple mediums instead of a single advertisement in the newspaper. Posting photos, videos, articles, and much more to social media helps us to share our lives with the people we love. We can communicate our thoughts and feelings in a variety of ways that were not available without current digital technology.

---

1 See Reid Chassiakos et al., "Children and Adolescents and Digital Media," e6.

2 See Reid Chassiakos et al., e6.

Finally, technology can increase our psychological health and wellness by raising our awareness of topics and issues.[3] Before technology, our viewpoints might have been influenced by what we read in our local newspaper or heard from others. The radio and TV provided greater exposure to topics and issues of which we were not aware. Now, technology allows us to interact with top news stories, communicate directly with eyewitnesses, hear opinions from both sides of an issue, and discover stories and ideas that do not always make national or international headlines. There is so much information at our fingertips that we can learn as much as we want about whatever topic we want, which can help us form opinions and make informed decisions concerning important issues.

Health Cautions

There are also physical and psychological health concerns with technology. There are several physical concerns that apply to all ages. The first is eye strain. Spending numerous hours in front of technological devices, whether our phones, video games, or television sets, can unnaturally strain and prematurely age our eyes. When our eyes are glued to a small screen for a long period of time, our eyes are focusing on a virtual reality that deprives them of practice focusing on long-range items, three-dimensional objects, and other real-life objects. The American Optometric Association encourages the "20-20-20 rule" when using technology for long periods of time: take a twenty-second break every twenty minutes to look at something twenty feet away.[4]

The same rule of thumb is probably beneficial concerning our physical posture and movement in relation to technological devices. When working or playing on a device, it is much too easy to stay put for a long time in whatever comfortable position we choose. Being sedentary for extended periods of time has been shown to have serious negative effects on one's health. Some of the long-term effects of sitting in the same position for hours each day include organ damage, leg disorders, mus-

---

3 See Reid Chassiakos et al., e6.

4 American Optometric Association, "Future Eye Health."

cle degeneration, back problems, and slower brain function.[5] When using technology, children in particular tend to use positions that are not good for long-term health. Lying on one's stomach or back while using a keyboard entails poor posture, which is not conducive to physical wellness. However, one factor we often forget is that few technological spaces are designed with children's proper positioning and comfort in mind. The computer mouse may be too far out of reach for little children. The chairs may be too big or too small. The arrangement of the furniture, devices, and room can significantly influence the physical toll technology use can take, especially on children.[6]

> ## ▶TECHNOLOGY AND SITTING*

When sitting and using technology, remember these guides:

Do not lean forward.
Relax your shoulders.
Keep feet flat on the floor.
Relax elbows to a ninety-degree angle.
Keep arms close to sides.
Place technology within reach of young users.

___
* Berkowitz and Clark, "Health Hazards of Sitting."

Sleep can also be negatively affected by too much technology use. Many of us are quite comfortable bringing our mobile devices directly into bed with us to look at right before we go to sleep. However, technology use right before bedtime has negative effects on our sleep when compared to a winding down bedtime routine without technology. The American Academy of Pediatrics points to studies that indicate that those who use technology right before bed can experience sleep disturbances and daytime dysfunction.[7] Additionally, feeling pressure to be available twenty-four hours a day—causing us to take our technology everywhere we go—can negatively affect sleep. How many of us check our email the moment new messages ding on our devices, even when it is not an appropriate time for us to respond? Since sleep is one of the most

___
5   See Berkowitz and Clark, "Health Hazards of Sitting."

6   See Pollock and Straker, "Technology in Schools," 789.

7   See Reid Chassiakos et al., "Children and Adolescents and Digital Media," e8.

important factors in helping children and young adults develop strong and healthy bodies, a high priority should be placed on helping children establish and maintain healthy sleep habits.

Recommendations for Children's Media Use[8]

- **Younger than 18 months**—Avoid screen media except for video-chatting.

- **18–24 months**—Video-chatting and short amounts of high-quality children's programming is permissible. Best for parents to watch with children and explain what they are viewing.

- **2–5 years**—Limit screen time to one hour per day, choosing only high-quality programming. Parents are encouraged to coview media in order to guide children's perception and understanding.

- **6 years and older**—Consistent time limits on media use and types of media. Establish plenty of time for physical activity, sleep, and other healthy behaviors.

- Designate media-free times (such as dinnertime) and media-free locations (such as the bedroom).

Finally, technology can have a negative psychological impact because it can increase exposure to risky behaviors, such as drug use, disordered eating, and cyberbullying.[9] There is some anonymity with technology, but the likelihood of engaging in these risky behaviors in real life is compounded by having easy access to it online. These behaviors are also being promoted and normalized through technology, which can put children and young adults in more danger than they would have been without technology. We must be cognizant of these risks and safe-

THINK ABOUT IT

- When is your technology use the heaviest? the lightest? What about your children or students?

- What types of digital media and technology do you use most frequently?

- How do these types of technology impact you physically, mentally, and psychologically?

---

8 American Academy of Pediatrics, "Recommendations for Children's Media Use."

9 See Reid Chassiakos et al., e8.

guard against the negative health issues inherent in too much technology use. The digital citizenship trait of health and wellness encourages us to reflect on technology use instead of becoming absorbed in it without thinking. As Christians, God is our first priority, not technology; this means that we reevaluate our technology usage to keep God at the forefront.

Reflection vs. Absorption

Digital technology and media constantly surround us. It is no longer confined to a specific room in the home or at school. Because digital technology and media connect us on a global scale, it takes just a click to get new or updated information on your social media feed, web browser, and so forth. For many, this information and its constant availability is so essential that we can't unplug from it.[10] This includes embedding information with hyperlinks to provide access to more and more information, connecting information to multimedia that expands upon the information, and essentially making content more and more interactive so there is no apparent "end." When you watch a video on YouTube, endless suggestions to similar content are provided to try and maintain your interest and use. Where does this all lead to? The possibility of complete absorption in digital technology and media.

There is inherent danger in becoming absorbed in technology to the point that it consumes our lives. For children, absorption affects not only their brains but also their social interactions. To begin, absorption with technology can chip away at "concentration and contemplation."[11] For example, the skills children learn and wire in their brains for handling longer pieces of reading materials (namely, books) are essentially rendered useless as they engage in more online material that rewards constant skimming and clicking from source to source. Similarly, Mari Swingle argues that "if a busy brain discovers easy stimulation, it will not discover creativity, from which all innovation and invention births."[12] Creative

---

10 See Carr, *The Shallows*, 9.

11 Carr, 6.

12 Swingle, *i-Minds*, 51.

potential may be lost if it is absorbed into material that rewards simple skills rather than the more complex skills inherent in being creative and overcoming boredom on your own.

Technology absorption becomes a problem when a person cannot stop using technology, when someone prefers it to time spent with people and other activities, or when the use begins to have consequences in different areas of life.[13] This type of technological interference may seem extreme. You may think you do not fall into this extreme category of absorption or that your students are not this extreme. However, perhaps you feel comfortable pulling out your mobile device when you are at a restaurant with others and there is a lull in the conversation. Perhaps you see a group of students sitting together and talking and there is constant back-and-forth between conversations and mobile device use. Multitasking is indeed a myth, however much one justifies being able to jump from task to task.[14] At what point did we begin to feel so comfortable accessing our technology devices in social situations, when boredom strikes, when we have some unstructured free time, or really any time of day?

Our best example of what to do when we are too absorbed in a task, habit, or technology comes from the Bible. In the Bible, we read about how Jesus often removed Himself from His disciples or the crowds in order to rest and spend time with His Father in prayer. Following this example, we can build in time for ourselves and our students to rest from the demands of this world and our technology. While there is pressure to integrate technology into teaching and learning, the goal is to make this meaningful and purposeful. While we strive to use technology effectively in the classroom, we must also teach our students that there are times not to use technology too. It would probably be frowned upon if people started pulling out their mobile devices in church. Why is that? Why is it okay to use digital devices in other social situations, but not in church? (Or is it not okay to use devices in other situations?) As teachers, we must

13 See Swingle, 8.

14 See Hamilton, "Think You're Multitasking?"

help students recognize those situations when using digital technology could distract from deeper connections with God and others.

If we are constantly absorbed in digital technologies, we tend to ignore everything else around us instead of stopping to think and reflect. Being absorbed in something is worthless without reflection. How do we make sense of what we have learned? How do we know what steps we need to take next? Part of the difficulty with digital technology is that the line is blurred between communication and entertainment.[15] A person can easily end a video game without reflecting on anything other than how to achieve the next level or beat the enemy. However, a person could walk away from a great conversation with a teacher, pastor, or mentor with a solution to a difficult problem. In these examples, it is easy to tell which is entertainment and which is communication. But sometimes the distinction is less clear. For example, communication and social media are often built into games. You can play an online game with your friend across town and talk via headsets. But this communication is likely not very productive for anything other than the game; its primary purpose is still entertainment. The factors in the table below can help when evaluating whether a technology is primarily for entertainment or communication.

Communication	Entertainment
A tangible result of some sort—whether it be services provided or relationships strengthened	Temporary in nature—both in time and perhaps benefits
Lesson learned, new understanding developed, some sort of awareness	No substantial learning takes place
Perhaps a move to action	Maybe a distraction or time-filler
Multiple people involved and perhaps benefits earned	Can be somewhat selfish or self-focused
Maybe high cognitive demand	Low cognitive demand

---

15 See Reid Chassiakos et al., "Children and Adolescents and Digital Media," e3.

"The type of media, the type of use, the amount and extent of use, and the characteristics of the individual child" are all factors in determining appropriate use of digital technology, whether for entertainment or communication.[16] We are not preaching against popping in a movie on Friday night for family time or playing computer games or watching something that makes us laugh. Those are valuable and sometimes necessary parts of our lives. What we are arguing here is that we should not blindly hand technology off to students or children with no expectations, direction, or contemplation. Are we comfortable with children spending hours on video games because they act as a babysitter? Consider Philippians 4:8: "Whatever is true, whatever is honorable, whatever is just, whatever is pure, whatever is lovely, whatever is commendable, if there is any excellence, if there is anything worthy of praise, think about these things." We must be thoughtful in how we present technology to students and children and how we expect them to use it by creating a shared experience to enable discussion and reflection.[17] This means we must be present in their lives and serve as positive role models.

BEING ROLE MODELS

While media is omnipresent in our lives and children seem to have instinctive abilities and understanding when it comes to using technology, children (and even some adults) need help learning boundaries and appropriate use. Mari Swingle argues, "Children still need mentors. Children need to debrief, and discuss the learning process, the views, and feelings of other individuals. . . . Something or someone has to encourage reflection."[18] As adults, we can usually pick up on how we are using technology. We know we really should not play video games for three hours at a time. We know there is a time to shut the technology off. Children, on the other hand, are still developing self-regulation skills and need mentors to intervene and teach them about using technology with intention.

---

16 Hill et al., "Media and Young Minds," 3.

17 See Hill et al., 4.

18 Swingle, *i-Minds*, 92.

It is our role as parents, guardians, or teachers to model sound technology use that promotes wellness in mind, body, and soul. Children and young adults need to see what is and is not appropriate media consumption and use. This means that we will have to decide what kind of role model we want to be. For example, if we think it is inappropriate to have technology out during conversations, meals, and so forth, then we, as role models, need to adhere to our own expectations. Technology should not be the only option for keeping children quiet when out in public spaces, when they get up early in the morning, or when they are full of energy. We may use technology to unwind by scrolling through our social media accounts, but if we want our children, students, or other youth to relax without technology, then we need to show them how to do it. Similarly, if we are so quick to pick up our phone every time it dings with an email or text message, then we are modeling that technology is the top priority in our lives.

The bottom line is that technology should not be a replacement for parents, teachers, and people in general. This does not mean technology needs to be viewed as a special treat or something evil. Rather, because technology is ever-present in our lives, we must model healthy ways to use it. We must orient our lives in such a way that technology is seen as a tool rather than as the centerpiece of our existence.

▶ **A DIGITAL MEDIA ROLE MODEL . . .**

puts away devices for specific reasons and asks that others do the same.

uses digital media for specific purposes, not just to "waste time" or to escape when bored.

explains to others how and why he or she uses technology for different purposes.

follows through on action plans to set limits on technology use or to have technology-free zones.

practices healthy behaviors that don't include digital devices and articulates to others the importance of doing so.

Orienting Our Lives

Colossians 3:1–2 says, "If then you have been raised with Christ, seek the things that are above, where Christ is, seated at the right hand of God. Set your minds on things that are above, not on things that are on earth." As Christians, we are to orient our lives toward Christ, but we so often fall short of this difficult calling. Taking time to confess, both in church and on our own, when our focus is on our own concerns rather than God's will can serve as a reminder that we need a Savior. We need a Savior to forgive us and reorient us when people, our jobs, and even technology consume our lives.

Part of being oriented toward Christ is examining the ways technology affects our lives, both physically and psychologically. Research shows that use of technology and media can harm us physically and psychologically when it "displaces physical activity, hands-on exploration, and face-to-face social interaction."[19] Human beings are holistic. God created our bodies, and He wants us to take care of them. He also wants us to authentically interact with and relate to the people around us. Therefore, we strive to establish an appropriate balance between technology consumption and healthy behaviors.

What would that appropriate balance look like? You can start to explore that question by tracking how much time you spend using technology and for what purposes in the course of a week. This can provide insight not only on the frequency of your technology use but also on how much of your technology use is required (such as for schoolwork or research) and how much is a personal choice (such as for entertainment or social interaction). Based on the data collected, start a conversation on what an appropriate balance is between technology and no technology. Also use this discovery to examine how often children's and young people's social interactions occur with technology or face-to-face. Reflect on how often technology serves as an interruption rather than an important

---

19 American Academy of Pediatrics, "Recommendations for Children's Media Use."

component to specific tasks. For next steps, develop a media plan that takes into account health, education, and entertainment.[20]

MEDIA PLAN*

Use the outline below to guide your classroom or family in conversation about tracking and planning your current and future media use. You may also want to create a chart with these headings and send it home with students to track their media use.

- Screen-free zones and times
  Where and when
- Choose and diversify media
  Cowatching and coviewing
  Not downloading bad apps or visiting bad sites
  What to do when using technology?
    Video-chatting
    Be creative
    Educational materials
- Balancing online and offline time
  Other recreational activities to engage in

- Remembering manners
  Putting devices away when talking with others
  No device out at certain times
- Safety
  Sharing with others
  Befriending others
  Not giving out personal information
- Digital citizenship
  Avoiding bullying
  Helping others
  Remembering the nine traits!
- Healthy behaviors
  Sleep
  Exercise

* American Academy of Pediatrics.

---

20 See American Academy of Pediatrics.

Physically speaking, there are numerous aspects to take into account to orient our use of technology toward Christ. Devorah Heitner describes focusing on the physical aspect of technology as creating a media ecology.[21] For example, if the goal is to get everyone to unplug more, then the most attractive areas in the home should not have technology in them. Instead, the goal is to create attractive unplugged zones. There should also be, in general, media-free zones in the house and the classroom.[22] In technology zones, make sure there is appropriate furniture to avoid health risks of poor physical posture while using technology.[23] Make it a goal to have technology and digital media be present and shared only in public spaces rather than private areas such as bedrooms where there is limited opportunity for monitoring and/or discussion.

The bottom line is that we need structure. Just as we must purposefully incorporate times and places where we engage with God's Word and prayer, we must also have structure with technology usage to promote health and wellness. Gene Veith asks us to consider this: How does technology and digital media help or hinder me in performing the duties of my vocation?[24] As teachers and adult role models, we cannot control what happens once students leave our classrooms. They may spend their bus ride home glued to their phones and then move to their bedrooms to watch TV all afternoon or play video games until dinner. Later, while they are doing their homework, they may be texting their friends, listening to music, watching TV, researching on the Internet, and so forth. We do not have control over this. But within our classrooms, we can help them to understand that just as we are purposeful about engaging with God, we must also be purposeful about engaging with technology. If children and young people pause to think about technology use, then at least we have accomplished something, even if the behavior does not always immediately follow!

---

21 Heitner, *Screenwise*, 111.

22 See Hill et al., "Media and Young Minds," 3.

23 See Bennett, "Child Use of Technology," 575.

24 Veith, "Technology and Vocation."

Classroom Lesson Plan

Well-Being in a World of Digital Technology

OVERVIEW

Because technology is so pervasive in our world, digital citizens must learn how to use technology in a way that does not cause physical damage. Parents, teachers, students, and others need to learn and practice technology usage that does not put too much strain on our eyes or joints and also learn to put down technology and be active to maintain healthy bodies.

BIG IDEA: **DIGITAL HEALTH AND WELLNESS**

ESSENTIAL QUESTIONS

- Are you always with your device (or on a screen)? How often do you check or look at it?

- When you have a free moment, where do your thoughts head first?

- When do you use your digital devices (or view your screen)? Is it in moments when you are alone? with someone?

STANDARDS OR GOALS

- Understand that being healthy includes more than just eating right.

ASSESSMENT

- Screen-time log

- Device-free period reflection

- Healthy technology statement

INSTRUCTIONAL MATERIALS

- Time log

- Word-processing program

INSTRUCTION

Stage 1

Students in classrooms have more screen time than in the past. Class discussion should begin with this topic: How many screens do you see in a day? How much time do you spend watching those screens? Students should estimate how many screens and how much time they spend each day and write this down at the top of the screen time log. Then students will be tasked with keeping track of how many screens and how much actual time they spend on screens in a day. They should take two days of log information and then take the average of the two days. When the logs come back, the class discussion should be centered on the pediatric recommendations for their age and the students' actual habits.

Stage 2

Because we spend considerable time on devices and screens, our thoughts often stray to those topics. As a class, discuss the many distractions in our lives (especially technology). The class will then begin a technology-free competition. The goal is for students to go at least twenty-four hours without using or viewing technology (including in the classroom). After the designated time period is over, the class will come back together to discuss how their technology-free time went. Then students will write a reflection on how easy or difficult the technology-free time was. Students can use any media for publishing their reflection, but a paper-and-pencil reflection might be appropriate considering the topic.

Stage 3

Healthy living advice is all around us. Many tools exist for healthy eating, such as nutrition labels or resources like ChooseMyPlate.gov. For technology though, definitive guidelines are less available. Students will craft a healthy technology statement, graphic, or motto that can be used for easy reference to use technology wisely.

Catechism Discussion Guide
Well-Being in a World of Digital Technology

BIG IDEA: **DIGITAL HEALTH AND WELLNESS**

ESSENTIAL QUESTIONS

- What are your priorities? How do you prioritize God and your faith?
- What does it mean to be physically and spiritually healthy?

CATECHISM FOCUS

1. ***First Commandment*** Students will demonstrate their understanding of God's plan for our lives to find our security and meaning in God alone and connect that to their digital behavior.

2. ***Third Commandment*** Students will demonstrate their understanding of how we should seek to hear God's Word in a digital age.

3. ***First Article of the Apostles' Creed*** Students will connect their understanding of how God the Father has created things for our use to how they use those created things to share the Gospel.

DISCUSSION POINTS

- What are your priorities in life? How do people see that?
- Do your online habits reflect your stated priorities?
- How do you put God first in all things? When you fail, what is your response? God's response?
- How can you honor God with your device time?
- How can we honor the Sabbath through technology?
- How can we improve our spiritual health with God's help?

- God's gift of technology can be healthy. How can you show that in your physical and digital life?

- How can technology help make you more spiritually healthy?

- God has created all things, even technology. How can we honor that gift in appropriate ways?

CHECK FOR UNDERSTANDING

- Individually or in pairs, direct students to develop a digital health and wellness plan for their lives. The format can be of the student's choosing. Examples might be a daily to-do list, a weekly or monthly calendar of activities, a daily prayer and Scripture-reading plan, or any combination of these. Student responses could be on paper, in their journals, built into their phone calendars, or dictated in a digital recording.

STUDENT VOICES

"We need to keep ourselves safe online."
DIGITAL SECURITY

"We need to keep ourselves safe online. One of the ways I can keep myself safe is to have an antivirus program on my laptop. We should keep our personal information safe and not give away our birth date or address and make our passwords difficult so that others cannot guess them. You also should not share your passwords with others. You should also never use your real name in a username because people could pretend to be you. While I was on a video game once, I had someone tell me that they were my friend, but they could not answer what my real name was, so I knew that they were fake. We should keep our photos safe by not letting others take or post pictures of us without our permission. It also helps to keep our name off of pictures, even though my mom and dad sometimes post pictures of me online. Sometimes we also need to use our intuition to keep us safe. If we think it is not right, then we should not click it. Sometimes things just look not right, and we should stay away from those places and never click on them."

QUESTIONS TO CONSIDER

1. How do you protect yourself in the digital world?

2. How often do you think about your safety online? Are you engaging in safe online habits?

3. How do you discern who is keeping you safe online? Which websites do you trust?

MOST PEOPLE IN the United States no longer consider it safe to leave their doors unlocked while they are away from home or asleep at night. It was not long ago that we did just the opposite. Growing up in rural Minnesota, my family rarely locked the house doors. Ever. I could walk into my grandparents' house at any time of the day or night. Not so today. Our homes are alarmed, have video security that can be accessed on our smartphones, and have sophisticated locks for keyless entry. Do we take the same precautions with our digital home?

In many ways, our smartphones, computers, and tablets are our "homes" today. For better or worse, our digital devices have information that is sensitive, personal, and meant only for ourselves or those close to us. We would never let a stranger into our home to browse through our valuables. Why, then, do we often leave our digital devices unlocked, use poor passwords, or allow others access?

Digital Security

Crimes like identity theft and fraud have been on the rise and continue to wreak havoc on individuals. Cyber criminals keep finding new and malicious ways to steal bank account information, social security numbers, and personal information. It might be more effective if our personal security was locked up in a vault; instead, most individuals leave personal information easily accessible.

THINK ABOUT IT

- Do you have a passcode set on your smartphone? How many people know what it is?

- How many different passwords do you use? Have you changed them lately?

- How many online accounts do you have? What information is stored there?

Maintaining digital security in our technology-heavy world is an everyday job that requires strict attention. Not only do we have to worry about personal devices and information stored there, but we must also remember that the devices in our professional world have private information too. Security is an abstract concept for students, and schools must find ways to make security concrete, visual, and as relevant as our own professional and personal digital safety.

SECURITY FOR DIGITAL NATIVES

The students we serve in our schools are all digital natives. They were born into a world that has always had digital technology. The technology they are accustomed to has been instant, personal, and accessible to them. Free Wi-Fi is available in many restaurants, retail stores, coffee shops, and businesses. Schools have Wi-Fi for staff, students, and guests. Digital access is everywhere, but are security measures in place everywhere?

Do you like cookies? If we are talking about the chocolate-chip kind, then probably yes! Do you know about digital cookies? In the digital world, cookies are used for tracking and obtaining information. Cookies are why you can be searching for Hawaiian vacations and then switch to a home-delivery shopping service and find swimsuits, suntan lotion, and sandals as automatic suggestions for purchase. Digital natives have always been a part of this interconnected digital experience, but that doesn't mean they know what information is being collected and whether that might compromise personal security.

The primary piece of information all digital users must know is that we are being tracked. Keystrokes, searches, clicks, and views are collected, analyzed, and used for a variety of purposes. Some tracking may make our lives easier; some may be more malicious. Social media sites are said to have the largest collection of facial recognition data in the world, which could be purchased at any time for a price. As long as we choose to use smartphones, smartwatches, and other personal technology devices, we will submit to tracking. Therefore, we must make sure we are aware of it and teach our students to make wise choices based on our knowledge about security.

MODELING WISE CHOICES WITH DIGITAL SECURITY

Besides parents, teachers are some of the most influential role models in students' lives. When we use digital technology with our students, we have the opportunity to model appropriate security measures so students learn how to keep themselves and others safe online. There are several ways teachers can do this. First, always talk about personal safety when using technology. Just as we talk about why we keep our bodies safe and modest, we need to be open with students about why we follow certain security measures—why we use passwords, why we do not tell people our passwords, and how to create passwords. For example, when students see you typing in a password for different accounts, tell them why the password is there. If students are logging in on a device, ask them about the reasons for having personal accounts and private information and what that means.

THINK ABOUT IT

- How do we currently help students make wise choices? Are wise behavioral choices in the physical world different from those in the digital world?

- Do students use a different decision-making process on digital devices than they do in the physical world (concerning friendships, for example)?

- What are adults modeling to students about making wise choices (digital or otherwise)?

Second, teach mini lessons on creating and protecting passwords. There is an art to password creation! Never use personal information in passwords—birthdays, our names or children's names, addresses. Think of unique phrases that are meaningful to you. Replace letters with numbers and symbols in the word or phrase (e.g., "bumbᴉebee"). Make passwords unique for each account so that if one is hacked, the criminal does not have access to all accounts. Students can have fun creating codes and passwords that are easy to remember, yet still feature proper security measures. Mention that passwords should be changed on a regular basis and that there are programs available to help store and keep track of the different passwords for our many accounts.

Third, share current events regarding digital security with students. While we do not want to create fear or panic, we do want students to understand that digital security is real and necessary, that there are nefarious activities that can compromise security and even ruin lives. Students as young as middle school can have robust discussion about hacking and cyber security.

Finally, students need to know that every time they get online, they are exposing themselves to digital risks; it is important for them to know how to behave appropriately to minimize those risks. Digital footprints can compromise their personal security. Sharing locations publicly could invite predators either in person or online. Our digital world is not going away, so we must be aware of the security risks and make wise choices to protect ourselves as much as possible.

Consider this learning situation: You have your computer connected to a projector, the class is watching you set everything up, and you have to quickly type in your password. As you type, some students see your password before the letters turn to circles, and they announce it to the class. "Why is your password 'Mr.FlutterBall'?!" You're busted! Instead of scolding the students or ignoring them, make this a teachable moment. Discuss when it is appropriate to change passwords—such as when someone discovers your password. What are other times? When you suspect you have been hacked or your information is compromised, change that password! Turn the students' quick wit into a mini lesson on digital security.

MODELING WISE CHOICES

1. Talk about personal safety.

- Plan discussion starters with your class.
- Observe what students are talking about and incorporate those discussions into class.

2. Teach mini lessons.

- Here are some potential topics:

  Passwords

  Different accounts

  Laws

  Bullying

  Talking with parents or adults

3. Share current events.

- Check news sources, YouTube, and other pop culture sites for current topics.
- Scan social media regularly to check what is popular with students.

4. Online exposure is risky.

- Model location security and talk about exposure. Sharing locations and allowing followers whom you do not know is dangerous.
- Have students share experiences; bring in experts to talk to students about cyber security.
- Keep up to date on these issues. They are constantly changing.

WISE CHOICES IN ACTION

Teachers are models in the classroom and in life. While we can model choices to our students all day long, it is still up to them to make good choices when no one is watching them. Internalizing what is safe and secure online behavior can be difficult. Consider this situation: Students take a digital literacy class in school where they talk, write, and view content about how to be safe online. When they leave the classroom, however, they may share their exact location on social media and use the same password for all of their accounts. There is a gap that needs to be bridged.

Another opportunity to model wise digital security is in regard to hacking. "In 2015, for instance, there were more than 177,866,236 personal records exposed via 780 data security breaches," and the statistics for 2017 were on par to break the 2015 numbers.[1] You or someone close to you has likely been a target of a hack. Just this year I have received three letters stating my personal information may have been compromised through a digital commerce site. Talk to your students about this dire situation. Save the letters from financial institutions or businesses that have warned you about data breaches. Show students the hacking statistics. Knowledge can encourage conscientious digital security habits.

Try This! The Identity Theft Resource Center has useful and current statistics on many forms of digital security. www.idtheftcenter.org/

Here are some interesting questions to ask of students who have social media: How many of the people who follow you on social media do you know personally? Do you know if everyone is who they say they are? Companies and some individuals are actually purchasing fake followers to boost their social media image.[2] A 2015 study estimated that 8 percent of all accounts on Instagram were fake.[3] Others may have more sinister intentions. "Online predators . . . do everything they can to trick children into thinking they're kids too. This means creating fake accounts and profiles. Not only do these predators create fake social media profiles, they also tend to populate the accounts with detailed information—creating an entirely new persona."[4] Sexual predators want to chat with children

---

1 DiGiacomo, "2017 Security Breaches."
2 See Wiltshire, "Fake Followers Epidemic."
3 Heath, "Fake Account Activity."
4 Kidguard, "Social Media and Online Predators."

and adolescents in order to collect sexually explicit photos from them or, worse, meet them in person. When students and parents are aware of the very real dangers of online predators and fake accounts, they can take action.

We want students to move beyond looking at their online security like they do algebra: "We're never going to use this in real life!" We need to use appropriate security measures every day. Several inquiry-based learning methods can be employed to help students think about their online security in real-life ways.

▶ IDENTIFYING FAKE SOCIAL MEDIA ACCOUNTS*

1. Read through the posts and profile of the suspected account. If you find only one-way conversation coming from it, without other people posting and interacting, it is probably fake.

2. Watch for spam coming from the account. If they do try to engage you, be wary of links or requests for wire transfers. This is a fake!

3. For high-profile users (e.g., celebrities, politicians), look for a verification of the social media accounts. Accounts for high-profile users without verification are likely fake.

4. Some profiles are created to give fake reviews of businesses or products. Do not follow any links they provide if the review seems absurdly slanted, has poor writing, or does not follow common grammatical conventions.

---

* Nikolai, "Spot a Social Media Fake."

Try This!

ONLINE SECURITY INQUIRY-BASED LEARNING

1. Look at real social media posts.

Rather than dealing in the hypothetical, engage students in real-life discussions about proper online security.

2. Practice what you preach.

Have students look at your social media presence. It may be difficult to allow students to see your online behavior, but this is the essence of modeling. Openly talk to students about why you make the choices you do online. What goes through your mind when you post or search online? Many of these discussions are best done with students in fifth grade and older, but the point is for full engagement and for students to see the real-life applications of appropriate online behavior.

3. Have a special speaker who is *not* an adult.

Students will listen to adults, but they take peers even more seriously. Invite a high school student to speak to your middle school students about social media, online temptations, and being safe online.

4. Be visible.

Encourage students to share their own social media posts, online habits, and struggles with the class. This is an incredibly vulnerable situation, but when trust is built in the classroom, this kind of an exchange of students' personal posts, habits, or struggles can flourish. Temptations can lead to poor online choices, which can lead to lapses in judgment that may compromise their digital security. Remember that as their teacher, you are a part of the community as well, so share your posts with the class too.

Digital Security Is More Than Passwords and Hacking

Online security is just as important as physical security, like locking doors or not talking to strangers. As teachers, it is part of our job to teach our students how to engage in the digital world according to their vocations, but to do so in safe and positive ways. However, we have to broaden the conversation beyond passwords and bank account information when it comes to security. Yes, we have security when we lock our front door and install firewalls on our computer, but more important, we have eternal security in our Baptism. In Christian schools, any talk about security should inevitably lead us to our source of true security: Jesus Christ. Things will go wrong, no matter how many passwords we have or security measures we take. While we use the resources we have to be as safe as possible and to educate our students, our ultimate trust is in Jesus to help us even when things go wrong in this world.

We have the privilege of proclaiming to the world that our ultimate and eternal security is found in the salvation bought for us by Jesus' life, death, and resurrection. We are given that security by the Holy Spirit; however, our digital world has desperately tried to shift the focus. Instead of focusing on Christ, the world wants us to find our security in what others are doing, liking, eating, and being. Instead of finding our security in God's Word, the world tries to find truth in philosophy, humanism, and popularity. The world is corrupted by sin and constantly distracts us from the Gospel message. But Christian schools and churches can help their students and members stay focused on the true security that Christ provides.

Here are some ways to focus your children and students on our eternal security in Christ in the midst of a digital world:

- Be aware of the digital influences all around. Rather than try to ignore the digital world, churches and schools should take advantage of the daily trends to focus on God in each situation. For example, instead of ignoring a major social rally that has trended on every social media platform, talk about it thoroughly and ask how can God be glorified in this situation. When students bring up something that a celebrity did, do not ignore it; use it as a way to talk to students about their security in Christ.

- Talk about identity. In Baptism, we were eternally saved and marked as God's own children. We need to continue to talk about this unique identity we have in all aspects of our ministries. Baptism is not a "once and done" activity; we need to continue to live out God's purpose and plan for us in our lives. Sermons, lessons, Bible studies, and prayers should always remind us of our identity as children of God.

- Confess and be forgiven. No matter how hard we try, we know that we are sinful and will fall short of God's perfect design for our lives. Our ultimate security lies in Jesus, whose sacrifice allows us to come to the Father and say, "I messed up and need You, Lord." We confess our need for Him who saved us and receive His perfect forgiveness.

▶ RESOURCES FOR DIGITAL SECURITY

Identity Theft Resource Center—statistics on cyber security. www.idtheftcenter.org/

Kidguard—digital monitoring. www.kidguard.com

Kids Live Safe—protecting children from sex offenders. www.kidslivesafe.com/

The world tries so hard to distract us from God's plan for us. While we may not be able to leave our doors unlocked or our accounts unprotected, we can practice safe digital habits that keep our digital identities secure. We can also rest in God's security of who we are in Him who saved us. Whether it is digital security or eternal security, we have all that we need in God the Father, Son, and Holy Spirit.

Classroom Lesson Plan
Electronic Safety Precautions

OVERVIEW

While it would be great if we could trust everyone online to do the right thing, that is not the case. The digital world contains safeguards meant to protect users from physical, psychological, and financial threats. All technology users must be familiar with these safeguards and implement them in the appropriate ways to keep themselves and those close to them safe.

BIG IDEA: **DIGITAL SECURITY**

ESSENTIAL QUESTIONS

- How do you protect yourself in the digital world?
- How many different passwords do you use? Have you changed them lately?
- How many online accounts do you have? What information is stored there?

STANDARDS OR GOALS

- Protecting yourself is important; diligently plan and implement proper safety measures.

ASSESSMENT

- Wisdom statement or reflection
- Rewrite Proverbs 2:1–5
- Public service announcement about digital safety

INSTRUCTIONAL MATERIALS

- Word-processing program
- Video recording and editing tools

INSTRUCTION

Stage 1

Start with a class discussion about what we can do to stay safe while online, and create a list of wise choices from the discussion. Using the list, students will create a digital security wisdom statement. This statement should reflect the challenges of online security and include actions the students can take to be safe online.

Stage 2

Have students carefully examine Proverbs 2:1–5, using various translations and commentaries. Then have them rewrite the passage to apply that wisdom in our digital lives.[5]

Stage 3

Having thought about making wise choices and the things that God gives us to make wise choices, students should record a public safety announcement (PSA) video targeted to their peers about keeping safe and making wise choices while online. Students can incorporate the list of wise choices developed in stage 1 into their PSA. Students should record and edit their video and then find a safe way to share their PSA with their peers (blog, vlog, video-sharing site). The videos should also incorporate ways to keep parents informed about online safety as well.

---

5 This is not meant to rewrite God's Word; rather, it is meant to provide students with a paraphrased verse that helps them think about making wise choices in a digital world.

Catechism Discussion Guide
Electronic Safety Precautions

BIG IDEA: DIGITAL SECURITY

ESSENTIAL QUESTIONS

- How do you protect yourself against sinful temptations?
- How can we be confident of our safety in all aspects of the world?
- How is our ultimate security already completed?

CATECHISM FOCUS

1. *Baptism* Students will summarize how God has given them security, identity, and meaning in their Baptism.

2. *The Lord's Prayer* Students will demonstrate an understanding of God's plan for us as His children and how we are to commend our lives to Him.

3. *The Apostles' Creed* Students will identify ways that each person of the Trinity gives a particular form of security.

DISCUSSION POINTS

- Through Baptism, we have been safely brought to eternal, saving faith in Jesus Christ. How can we confidently share that safety in any platform?

- Even though we are saved by God's grace in the waters of Baptism, evils of the world still exist. How does our faith help us resist the temptations of the devil?

- We pray that we would not be led into temptation. What online safeguards has God provided to keep us out of harm's way? What in-person safeguards has God provided to protect us online?

- How are adults around us an answer to the prayer "deliver us from evil"?

- The Father, Son, and Holy Spirit all are part of our spiritual and physical security. Identify ways that each person of the Trinity keeps us safe (online or physically).

- God the Father has created us, Jesus has saved us, and the Holy Spirit has brought us to faith and daily renews our souls. How can this ultimate security be shared and visible in our digital lives?

CHECK FOR UNDERSTANDING

- After the group discussion, split students into pairs or trios and give each group a question from above. Ask them to dig a little deeper than the group's initial discussion and add at least two ideas to the conversation about that question. After a given amount of time, groups will share their ideas with the class as a whole.

- As a culminating activity, ask students to respond with both words and drawings in their daily journal. Translating their words into pictures will help them to think more deeply about the concepts they are internalizing.

> "Keep God at the forefront of our thoughts when online."

DIGITAL FAITH LEADERS

"God's Word tells us to treat others the way we would want to be treated. It is the Golden Rule. We should be like Jesus and do what He would want us to do online with others. With this in mind, being a digital faith leader means being nice and leading by example, like on social media. If we are following God's laws, it should show others that we are Christians. You should not post things that others do not want you to. If you are a believer, you will not do that. If you are a Christian, you do not go around and say bad things about others. Our faith and what we do in all areas of our lives, especially online, should not be separated. One way to keep them together is by thinking about what Jesus would want us to do. We do not have to follow the crowd if others are doing a bunch of bad things, and we should stick up for others if they cannot do it themselves."

Faith in the Digital World:
From Citizens to Leaders

THE NINE TRAITS of digital citizenship serve as a blueprint or foundation for a larger discussion to be had at home, in the classroom, in parish education, and when collaborating with others concerning digital practices. While each trait and biblical principle can be taught or discussed in isolation from one another or as pieces of the larger picture of digital citizenship, Mike Ribble provides groupings of the traits for a more interconnected view:[1]

- Respect yourself and others
    - Digital etiquette
    - Digital law
    - Digital access

- Educate yourself and others
    - Digital literacy
    - Digital communication
    - Digital commerce

- Protect yourself and others
    - Digital health and wellness
    - Digital rights and responsibilities
    - Digital security

For example, in a conversation about respecting yourself and others with the use of digital technology, we could discuss how what we post online and say about others might affect them personally despite our intentions (digital etiquette). We might discuss how not everyone has the

---

1 Ribble, *Digital Citizenship in Schools*, 57–58.

same privileges of getting the newest gadgets to stay cutting edge in their practices (digital access). We might end the conversation about respecting ourselves and others by discussing the importance of giving credit to others for ideas rather than taking them for ourselves (digital law).

Similarly, when talking about educating ourselves and others, students could learn the different skills needed to navigate and make sense of what they find online (digital literacy), which would naturally extend into examining and understanding what they actually do online (digital communication). These conversations would branch off into different areas with a particular focus on how to be safe when buying and selling online (digital commerce). Since safety is paramount, we could end the conversation with a focus on protection, learning how to care for ourselves physically and mentally while using digital technology (digital health and wellness) as well as how to protect our identity (digital security). All of this could be framed by understanding what we can and cannot do online, making sure that what we do is appropriate not only for ourselves but for others too (digital rights and responsibilities). Respect, meaningful learning, and protection are focal points in any educational curriculum, and extending these ideas into the digital realm with a framework makes it easier for students to make connections and see the relevance in their own lives.

Another way to group the nine digital citizenship traits is according to the biblical traits that have been integrated and connected throughout this book:

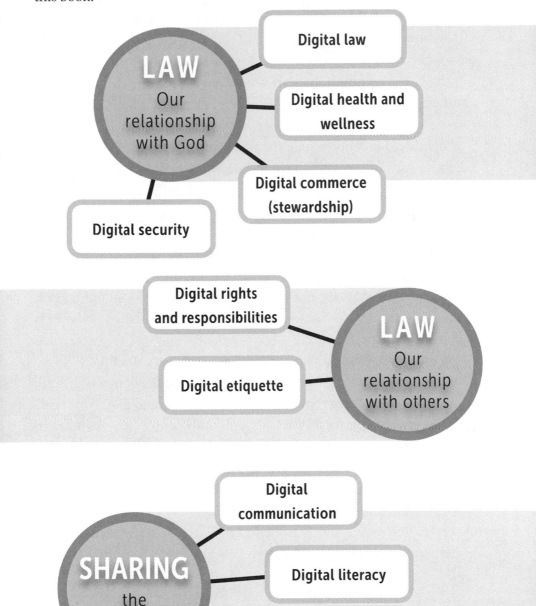

For example, framing the Bible in terms of Law and Gospel points to our sinful nature and the need for a Savior. Understanding digital citizenship in terms of Law and Gospel also points to our need for Jesus. Have a conversation about the different ways information can be stolen online and what the consequences are (digital law), or discuss how to protect ourselves and others from online scams (digital security). Law and Gospel can also be used to think about the freedoms we possess in a digital world and how we can best use and share these freedoms (digital rights and responsibilities).

After this foundational understanding, you can move into using technology to care for others by being a cheerful giver (digital stewardship) and caring for the physical and mental well-being of others (digital health and wellness) while also not bearing false witness or slandering others online (digital etiquette). Finally, just as in everyday life, our sharing of the Gospel should also extend into our digital lives. This includes understanding the different ways to communicate the Gospel (digital communication), the skills we must know to accomplish this important task (digital literacy), and making sure that we spread the Gospel to the ends of the earth (digital access).

As you can see from the groupings and from the overall idea of students and young people being active participants in the digital realm, the goal is for young people to see themselves as more than digital bystanders. Instead, we advocate for students and young people to be digital faith citizens. Citizenship implies that students and young people have the opportunity to shape the culture and community to which they belong. By living out the biblical principles connected with each trait, students move beyond compliance and awareness. Students should know how to use technology appropriately and understand that it is a gift from God to be used wisely in all contexts.

Types of Citizenship

Citizenship by itself is tricky to define, as it contains different meanings in different contexts, and defining a digital faith citizen is no different. However, a digital faith citizen recognizes the importance of integrating biblical principles into all areas of life, especially when dealing with technology and digital media. But how exactly do we do that? Joel Westheimer and Joseph Kahne offer three common types of citizenship: personally responsible, participatory, and justice oriented.[2] Personally responsible citizenship is what most of us think of: a person who is mindful of the community and world he or she lives in by recycling, donating to charitable causes, and voting. Personally responsible citizenship is also connected to traditional character education and promoting ideals such as honesty, loyalty, and fairness.

Participatory citizenship takes personally responsible citizenship to the next level by focusing on engagement. Rather than staying isolated or focusing on oneself, participatory citizens plan and organize community-based efforts and are more involved in general. Similarly, justice-oriented citizenship is also involved in engagement, but rather than simply organizing, these types of citizens spend time analyzing and reflecting on social, economic, and political forces that are affecting the community. They are more concerned with social movements and effecting change.

CITIZENSHIP TYPES

PERSONALLY RESPONSIBLE——PARTICIPATORY——JUSTICE-ORIENTED

How do you demonstrate the various types of citizenship in your own life?

What type of citizenship is demonstrated by your students?

Are any of these directly taught?

How does God's design and plan of salvation
play into these citizenship types?

The goal of any of these types of citizenship is to gain skills to benefit the community in some way. For example, students may gain awareness of the types of skills needed to be a personally responsible citizen, such

---

2 Westheimer and Kahne, "What Kind of Citizen?," 237.

as learning how to locate food banks in a community and determining what type of donations they accept. Participatory citizens might learn to assist in food or clothing drives, learn how to write grants to secure funds for different events, or learn the logistics of working with a city government to secure appropriate permits for events. Justice-oriented citizens might learn the best ways to lead conversations with different community members, how to research social phenomena and trace the histories of different social movements, and how to examine and change policies embedded in government.

One type of citizenship is not recommended over the others. However, the context contributes greatly to the type of citizenship that is promoted and studied. Most important for schools and churches is to have a clear goal and vision of the type of citizen students should be in your specific context. With this in mind, we recognize that bringing digital citizenship into schools and attaching biblical principles is as much about awareness and understanding as anything else.

The nine digital citizenship traits and the integrated biblical principles form a foundation for future thought, discussion, actions, and habits. Digital knowledge should lead to good habits, just as our faith should be lived out and shared daily. Although this is not easy to accomplish, the best way to make progress is to infuse digital citizenship and faith in every part of your school and church where technology intersects. Once students have a clear grasp on the traits and can reflect on their digital identities and how they navigate the digital realm in a faith-based way, we encourage you not to stop your efforts there. Students should not only be personally responsible digital faith citizens but be digital faith leaders as well.

What Is Digital Faith Leadership?

Thus far we have discussed digital citizenship as using digital media in a responsible and ethical way. Author George Couros defines digital leadership as "using the vast reach of technology (especially . . . social media) to improve the lives, well-being, and circumstances of others."[3] To take it a step further, digital faith leadership would be using digital media to spread the Gospel, show compassion and care for others as Jesus would do, and generally focus on the idea of improving the lives of others. The goal of digital faith leadership is to move beyond thinking only of self—what do *I* need to do and what is happening with *me*. As digital faith leaders, we must focus on our community, near or far. Using technology to care for people in our church, school, social group, mission plant, or adopted overseas organization is all part of being a digital faith leader.

What are some actions of a digital faith leader? One word that comes to mind when defining a digital faith leader is *inspirational*.[4] Being inspirational means focusing on the elements of continual learning in a digital environment and sharing that learning with others. It is quite easy to use digital media for somewhat selfish purposes, to play video games or shop online or talk with our friends. However, with endless information at our fingertips, we can do more and serve others through digital media by continually learning and sharing that knowledge with others. Additionally, what we learn in Bible or catechism instruction and celebrating our faith development can transform our actions and thoughts about digital media.

Digital leadership also includes empowering others who have no voice—those who are afraid to share stories, who do not have the luxury of technology, or who have not been represented accurately or at all in digital media. Most democracies allow citizens to worship how they please and share their faith openly; but for many Christians around the world, being open about their faith leads to persecution. Sharing their stories and giving voice to those who are suffering is important. As Christians, we are called to serve our neighbor, and the digital realm gives us many opportunities to do so.

The Bible makes it clear that the Gospel is for everyone. Acts 10 tells the story of Peter, filled with the Holy Spirit, preaching to the Gentiles;

---

3 Couros, "Digital Leadership Defined."

4 See Heick, "Digital Citizenship to Digital Leadership."

the result was that "the gift of the Holy Spirit was poured out even on the Gentiles" (v. 45). Digital faith leaders have technology at their fingertips to bring God's Word to the ends of the earth. This gift and responsibility must not be taken lightly, but instead be used to further God's kingdom.

Digital faith leadership also means promoting important causes—such as societal inequalities or biblical principles on life, sexuality, and culture. This could mean doing food drives, clothing drives, service events, parent education, and other school-based events. Digital media provides a platform to do much more than just meet our own needs. We should be engaging with the community and discussing or promoting issues that are often ignored or overlooked.

Perhaps most important, digital leadership means using digital media to be a positive influence in the lives of others. This is a great opportunity to discuss servant leadership. Servant leadership means putting others first and thinking first of others' needs. It means forming relationships with others to learn about them rather than leading from the front, and gathering input from everyone involved. Service is the key when we move from citizenship to leadership. We want to change the world for Christ! Through the Holy Spirit, our goal is for students to have many and varied service opportunities, be inspired by others, and know that they can effect change with God's help. Servant leadership for students may begin small, but it is a critical piece of mission and vocation.

Mission and Vocation

Earlier in the book, there was an activity to review the mission statement of your church or school and bring it into the twenty-first century by seeing how well it did and did not fit into a digital setting. Even if no revisions are planned to include technology, the goal of the activity was to examine how the institution's mission is carried out while students are online.

MISSION STATEMENTS

Try This!

Examine each mission statement below. How could they be infused with digital faith citizenship?

1. St. John's mission to create disciples of Jesus Christ:

CONNECT to God and His people in Worship.

GROW together in God's Word through Life Groups.

SHARE Christ with our Words, Service, and Resources. *

- **Possible questions to ask:** How do we connect? Is worship available online? Are there any digital Life Groups? Do we share in a technological sense?

---

2. As we align our vision for Redeemer with God's vision for us, we pray that Redeemer will:

grow larger not for the sake of being bigger, but to broaden our impact, our outreach, the breadth and depth of our ministry, in order to lead a growing number of people into a life-changing relationship with Jesus.

grow deeper in our love for God and others as we encourage each person to take the next step toward spiritual maturity. We will grow deeper in our spiritual practices, relationships with each other, and our passion to be Jesus' disciples.

grow deeper in developing a culture of generosity. Blessed to bless others; changed lives to change lives!

reach a new generation with the Gospel message, inspiring and empowering them to lead the church of today and tomorrow as they meet needs and change lives through Jesus Christ. **

---

* St. John's Lutheran Church of Orange, "What We Believe," www.stjohnsorange.org.

** Redeemer Lutheran Church, "About," www.redeemer.net.

MISSION STATEMENTS CONTINUED

- **Possible questions to ask:** Are we reaching a new generation with new technology? Is spiritual maturity linked to technology in any way? Can we be more generous with digital stewardship of resources?

3. St. Luke's is a thriving community of believers in Jesus Christ proclaiming His name in everything that we do. By God's grace alone, St. Luke's exists to awaken and nurture thriving relationships with God through faith in Jesus Christ.***

- **Possible questions to ask:** Is the Word of God proclaimed in a digital manner? What kind of relationships are valued: face-to-face or online or a blend?

*** St. Luke's Lutheran Church and School, "Home," http://stlukes-oviedo.org/.

Of course, this mission should be connected to the Great Commission as found in Matthew 28:19–20: "Go therefore and make disciples of all nations, baptizing them in the name of the Father and of the Son and of the Holy Spirit, teaching them to observe all that I have commanded you. And behold, I am with you always, to the end of the age." This Great Commission is difficult to achieve without moving from basic digital citizenship to digital leadership. Finding opportunities to be proactive in how we accomplish this great mission will show children and young adults that we cannot simply wait and hope that someone comes up to us and asks us to tell them about Jesus.

Similarly, once we have examined our different vocations both offline and online, we can then begin to find opportunities to become digital leaders and servant leaders. Our different vocations provide many areas for students to explore their leadership potential. This could begin by identifying the different leadership roles and responsibilities inherent in the different vocations and then discussing how they can be extended into a digital setting.

THE GOAL IS ETERNITY

In all that we do as students, teachers, pastors, or parents, we learn, lead, and love out of motivation from Jesus. Since creation, God has called His people to worship Him and devote our lives to Him. Our sinful nature and the sinful world puts up roadblocks. Some would consider technology and our digital environment one of those roadblocks. We see the digital world as an opportunity not just to grow in our faith, but to truly transform how we, with the Holy Spirit's guidance, can model and share the saving Gospel message with the world.

Biblical principles for digital citizenship should not be only a means to an end, but a part of the path toward eternity in heaven with our Father.

> Do not be deceived, my beloved brothers. Every good gift and every perfect gift is from above, coming down from the Father of lights, with whom there is no variation or shadow due to change. Of His own will He brought us forth by the word of truth, that we should be a kind of firstfruits of His creatures. (James 1:16–18)

THINK ABOUT IT

- How is your vocation as a teacher different in the digital world?
- How is your vocation as a son or daughter different with technology?
- Are certain vocations more difficult because of technology? Are some easier? Why?
- How can technology make leading easier? Can it make leadership harder?
- What new vocations have sprung up because of technology? How could they be infused with biblical principles?

Since creation, God has provided His good gifts for His children, and technology is no different. The rich digital resources we have are a created gift from God and deserve concerted attention so they are not misused. Digital citizenship does not earn us salvation; however, when we use it wisely, this gift from God can be part of our outreach efforts and help keep our minds focused on His message.

In all of our digital interactions, we want others to see our faith shine through the milieu of corrupt thoughts and deeds. Our access to digital resources has brought us into digital citizenship. Jesus, through Baptism and the Word, has brought us into faith citizenship. We are truly digital faith citizens. May our posts, pictures, comments, likes, and shares point others toward our Savior, the source and perfecter of our faith.

Acknowledgments

From an abstract idea initiated at a conference to a published book, this process has been an exciting journey! This book is for all those in Christian education, whether it be in a church or school, who are struggling with the deluge of technology in our children's world. We hope that the ideas presented will help frame conversations and spur action from parents and children alike.

Jake would like to thank Ben for his patience and persistence throughout the process and for remaining his friend through it all. Jake's wife, Brooke, who is ever patient and loving, has been his constant supporter and encourager!

Ben would like to thank Jake for meeting Ben's self-imposed deadlines and for (hopefully) enjoying the process. Ben could not have written this book or essentially function in life without his loving wife, Robyn, who is his constant supporter and to whom he is grateful for joining him in this wonderful journey called life.

To God be the glory!

Bibliography

Adams, Dennis M., and Mary Hamm. *Literacy in a Multimedia Age*. Norwood, MA: Christopher-Gordon, 2001.

American Academy of Pediatrics. "American Academy of Pediatrics Announces New Recommendations for Children's Media Use." October 21, 2016. https://www.aap.org/en-us/about-the-aap/aap-press-room/Pages/American-Academy-of-Pediatrics-Announces-New-Recommendations-for-Childrens-Media-Use.aspx.

American Optometric Association. "The 21st Century Child: Increased Technology Use May Lead to Future Eye Health and Vision Issues." July 28, 2015. http://www.aoa.org/newsroom/the-21st-century-child-increased-technology-use-may-lead-to-future-eye-health-and-vision-issues?sso=y.

Bajus, Mark. "Do People Read Your Content? 6 Facts about Reading Online." *Trapit Blog*, April 15, 2014. http://blog.trap.it/blog/bid/382592/Do-People-Read-Your-Content-6-Facts-about-Reading-Online.

Baker, Frank W. "Students Need Our Help Detecting Fake News." MiddleWeb, November 20, 2016. https://www.middleweb.com/33386/students-need-our-help-detecting-fake-news/.

Bennett, Cheryl L. "Child Use of Technology at Home." In *Ergonomics for Children: Designing Products and Places for Toddler to Teens*, edited by Rani Lueder and Valerie J. Berg Rice, 573–604. Boca Raton, FL: Taylor and Francis Group, 2007.

Berg, Judy. "Stewardship for Children." Stewardship Resources, LCMS.org, 2014. https://www.lcms.org/how-we-serve/national/stewardship-ministry/resources.

Berkowitz, Bonnie, and Patterson Clark. "The Health Hazards of Sitting." *Washington Post*. January 20, 2014. https://www.washingtonpost.com/apps/g/page/national/the-health-hazards-of-sitting/750/.

Carr, Nicholas. *The Shallows: What the Internet Is Doing to Our Brains*. New York: W. W. Norton and Company, 2011.

Chase, Zac, and Diana Laufenberg. "Embracing the Squishiness of Digital Literacy." *Journal of Adolescent and Adult Literacy* 54, no. 7 (2011): 535–37.

Cohen, Peter, and Jeff Livingston. "More Than Half of U.S. Schools Don't Have Adequate Wireless Access." *The Atlantic*, November 13, 2013. https://www.theatlantic.com/education/archive/2013/11/more-than-half-of-us-public-schools-dont-have-adequate-wireless-access/281410/.

Coiro, Julie, and Elizabeth Dobler. "Exploring the Online Reading Comprehension Strategies Used by Sixth-Grade Skilled Readers to Search for and Locate Information on the Internet." *Reading Research Quarterly* 42, no. 2 (2007): 214–57.

Couros, Alec, and Katia Hildebrant. "What Kind of (Digital) Citizen?" *Open Thinking* (blog), June 5, 2017. https://educationaltechnology.ca/tag/activecitizenship.

Couros, George. "Digital Leadership Defined." *The Principal of Change* (blog), January 7, 2013. https://georgecouros.ca/blog/archives/3584.

Creedon, Anthony. "Stewardship for Youth." Stewardship Resources, LCMS.org, 2014. https://www.lcms.org/how-we-serve/national/stewardship-ministry/resources.

DiGiacomo, John. "2017 Security Breaches: Frequency and Severity on the Rise," Revision Legal. Accessed June 20, 2017. https://revisionlegal.com/data-breach/2017-security-breaches/.

Enough Is Enough. "Pornography." Accessed May 21, 2017. http://enough.org/stats_porn_industry.

Federal Communications Commission. "E-Rate: Universal Service Program for Schools and Libraries." Consumer Guides. Last modified October 27, 2017. https://www.fcc.gov/consumers/guides/universal-service-program-schools-and-libraries-e-rate.

———."Fact Sheet: Update of E-Rate for Broadband in Schools and Libraries." Commission Documents. July 19, 2013. https://www.fcc.gov/document/fact-sheet-update-e-rate-broadband-schools-and-libraries.

Fertik, Michael, and David Thompson. *The Reputation Economy*. New York: Crown Business, 2015.

Goldman, David. "Music's Lost Decade: Sales Cut in Half." CNNMoney.com, updated February 3, 2010. http://money.cnn.com/2010/02/02/news/companies/napster_music_industry/.

Grayson, Robert. *Managing Your Digital Footprint*. New York: Rosen, 2011.

Hamilton, Jon. "Think You're Multitasking? Think Again." *NPR*, October 2, 2008. https://www.npr.org/templates/story/story.php?storyId=95256794.

Heath, Alex. "Instagram Is Starting to Crack Down on Fake Account Activity." Business Insider, April 20, 2017. http://www.businessinsider.com/instagram-cracks-down-on-fake-accounts-by-shutting-down-instagress-2017-4.

Heick, Terry. "Moving Students from Digital Citizenship to Digital Leadership." TeachThought. Accessed June 17, 2017. http://www.teachthought.com/the-future-of-learning/digital-citizenship-the-future-of-learning/moving-students-from-digital-citizenship-to-digital-leadership/.

Heitin, Liana. "How Should Reading Be Taught in a Digital Era?" *Education Week*, November 8, 2016. https://www.edweek.org/ew/articles/2016/11/09/how-should-reading-be-taught-in-digital-era.html.

Heitner, Devorah. *Screenwise: Helping Kids Thrive (and Survive) in Their Digital World*. Brookline, MA: Bibliomotion, Inc., 2016.

Hemmer, Jeff. "Grace and Every Blessing: The Gifts Hidden in the Commandments." Stewardship Resources, LCMS.org, 2014. https://www.lcms.org/how-we-serve/national/stewardship-ministry/resources.

Hill, David, Nusheen Ameenuddin, Yolanda Reid Chassiakos, Corinn Cross, Jeffrey Hutchinson, Alanna Levine, Rhea Boyd, Robert Mendelson, Megan Moreno, and Wendy Sue Swanson. "Media and Young Minds." *Pediatrics* 138, no. 5 (November 2016).

Hobbs, Renee. *Digital and Media Literacy: Connecting Culture and Classroom*. Thousand Oaks, CA: Corwin Press, 2011.

Kidguard. "Social Media and Online Predators: Different Ways Online Predators Approach Victims." January 23, 2017. https://www.kidguard.com/cell-phone-monitoring-and-gps-tracking/social-media-online-predators-different-ways-online-predators-approach-victims/.

Knolhoff, Wayne. "The Accountable Steward." Stewardship Resources, LCMS.org, 2014. https://www.lcms.org/how-we-serve/national/stewardship-ministry/resources.

Lenhart, Amanda, Oliver Lewis, and Lee Rainie. "Part 3: Teens and Their Schools." Pew Research Center, June 21, 2001, http://www.pewinternet.org/2001/06/21/part-3-teens-and-their-schools/.

Leu, Donald J., Lisa Zawilinski, Elena Forzani, and Nicole Timbrell. "Best Practices in Teaching the New Literacies of Online Research and Comprehension." In *Best Practices in Literacy Instruction*, 3rd ed., edited by Linda B. Gambrell, Lesley Mandel Morrow, and Michael Pressley, 343–64. New York: Guilford Press, 2007.

Maguth, Brad M. "The Educative Potential of Cell Phones in the Social Studies Classroom." *The Social Studies* 104, no. 2 (2013): 87–91.

McClintock, Pamela. "Kids at R-Rated Movies? Not If They're Under 6." *The Hollywood Reporter*, March 17, 2016. http://www.hollywoodreporter.com/news/kids-at-r-rated-movies-875627.

MediaSmarts. "Cyber Security Consumer Tip Sheet." Accessed August 2, 2017. http://mediasmarts.ca/tipsheet/cyber-security-consumer-tip-sheet.

———. "How to Recognize False Content Online—The New 5 Ws." Accessed June 23, 2017. http://mediasmarts.ca/teacher-resources/how-recognize-false-content-online-new-5-ws.

———. "Marketing and Consumerism—Overview." Accessed April 17, 2017. http://mediasmarts.ca/marketing-consumerism/marketing-and-consumerism-overview.

Middendorf, Michael P. *Romans 1–8*. St. Louis: Concordia Publishing House, 2013.

Nikolai, Aksana. "How to Spot a Social Media Fake." *Houston Chronicle*. Accessed August 14, 2017. http://smallbusiness.chron.com/spot-social-media-fake-46150.html.

Oxford Dictionaries. "Word of the Year 2016 Is . . ." Oxford University Press. Accessed December 29, 2016. https://en.oxforddictionaries.com/word-of-the-year/word-of-the-year-2016.

Paul, Annie Murphy. "Why Schools' Efforts to Block the Internet Are So Laughably Lame." *Slate*, July 1, 2014. http://www.slate.com/articles/technology/future_tense/2014/07/banned_website_awareness_day_why_schools_efforts_to_block_the_internet_are.html.

Perrin, Andrew, and Maeve Duggan. "Americans' Internet Access: 2000–2015." Pew Research Center, June 26, 2015. http://www.pewinternet.org/2015/06/26/americans-internet-access-2000-2015/.

Pollock, Clare, and Leon Straker. "Information and Communication Technology in Schools." In *Ergonomics for Children: Designing Products and Places for Toddler to Teens*, edited by Rani Lueder and Valerie J. Berg Rice, 783–800. Boca Raton, FL: Taylor and Francis Group, 2007.

Prensky, Marc. "Digital Natives, Digital Immigrants: Part 1." *On the Horizon* 9, no. 5 (September/October 2001): 1, 3–6.

Prigg, Mark. "Apple Ordered to Pay Back $32.5M for Accidental In-App Purchases—but Claims Decision 'Doesn't Feel Right.'" *Dailymail.com*, January 15, 2014. http://www.dailymail.co.uk/sciencetech/article-2540221/Apple-ordered-pay-32-5m-accidental-app-purchases.html.

Ramasubbu, Suren. "Biological and Psychological Reasons for Social Media Addiction." *Huffington Post*, updated March 13, 2017. https://www.huffingtonpost.com/entry/biological-psychological-reasons-for-social-media_us_58c279a7e4b0c3276fb78388.

Reid Chassiakos, Yolanda, Jenny Radesky, Dimitri Christakis, Megan A. Moreno, and Corinn Cross. "Children and Adolescents and Digital Media." *Pediatrics* 138, no. 5 (November 2016).

Recording Industry Association of America. "The True Cost of Sound Recording Piracy to the U.S. Economy." Facts and Research. Accessed December 12, 2017. https://www.riaa.com/reports/the-true-cost-of-sound-recording-piracy-to-the-u-s-economy/.

Ribble, Mike. *Digital Citizenship in Schools*. 3rd edition. Eugene, OR: International Society for Technology in Education, 2015.

———. "Home Page." Digital Citizenship: Using Technology Appropriately (website). Accessed May 21, 2017. http://www.digitalcitizenship.net.

Roesler, Jill. *Your Digital Footprint*. North Mankato, MN: Peterson Publishing Company, 2016.

Schilling, David Russell. "Knowledge Doubling Every 12 Months, Soon to Be Every 12 Hours." IndustryTap, April 19, 2013. http://www.industrytap.com/knowledge-doubling-every-12-months-soon-to-be-every-12-hours/3950.

Smaldino, Sharon, James D. Russell, Robert Heinich, and Michael Molenda. *Instructional Media and Technologies for Learning*. 7th ed. New York: Prentice Hall, 2001.

Strickland, Jonathan. "How Google Works." *HowStuffWorks.com*, December 20, 2006. http://computer.howstuffworks.com/internet/basics/google.htm.

Swingle, Mari K. *i-Minds: How Cell Phones, Computers, Gaming, and Social Media Are Changing Our Brains, Our Behavior, and the Evolution of Our Species*. Gabriola Island, BC: New Society Publishers, 2016.

Tapscott, Don. *Grown Up Digital: How the Net Generation Is Changing Your World*. New York: McGraw Hill, 2009.

Texas Education Agency. "Chapter 110: English Language Arts and Reading." Texas Essential Knowledge and Skills. http://ritter.tea.state.tx.us/rules/tac/chapter110/ch110b.html.

Ulrich, Larry. "Encouraging Generous Stewards." Stewardship Resources, LCMS.org, 2014, 2. https://www.lcms.org/how-we-serve/national/stewardship-ministry/resources.

Veith Jr., Gene Edward. *God at Work: Your Christian Vocation in All of Life*. Wheaton, IL: Crossway, 2002.

———. "Technology and Vocation." *The Lutheran Witness*, February 2011. https://blogs.lcms.org/2011/technology-vocation-2-2011.

Westheimer, Joel, and Joseph Kahne. "What Kind of Citizen? The Politics of Educating for Democracy." *American Educational Research Journal* 41, no. 2 (Summer 2004): 237–69.

Wiltshire, Crys. "The Fake Followers Epidemic." gShift, May 25, 2017. https://www.gshiftlabs.com/social-media-blog/the-fake-followers-epidemic/.

Yannuzzi, Thomas J., and Daniela Martin. "Voice, Identity, and the Organizing of Student Experience: Managing Pedagogical Dilemmas in Critical Classroom Discussions." *Teaching in Higher Education* 19, no. 6 (2014): 709–20.